Emerging Markets

Emerging Markets

Past and Present Experiences, and Future Prospects

Edited by

Sima Motamen-Samadian

and

Celso Garrido

First published in Great Britain 2000 by
MACMILLAN PRESS LTD
Houndmills, Basingstoke, Hampshire RG21 6XS and London
Companies and representatives throughout the world

A catalogue record for this book is available from the British Library.

ISBN 0–333–75343–7

First published in the United States of America 2000 by
ST. MARTIN'S PRESS, INC.,
Scholarly and Reference Division,
175 Fifth Avenue, New York, N.Y. 10010

ISBN 0–312–22898–8

Library of Congress Cataloging-in-Publication Data
Emerging markets : past and present experiences, and future prospects / edited by Sima Motamen-Samadian, Celso Garrido.
p. cm.
Includes bibliographical references and index.
ISBN 0–312–22898–8 (cloth)
1. Developing countries—Economic policy. 2. Structural adjustment (Economic policy)—Developing countries. 3. Financial crises—Developing countries. 4. Capital movements—Developing countries. I. Motamen-Samadian, Sima. II. Garrido N., Celso.
HC59.7.E48 1999
332'.09172'4—dc21 99–39493
CIP

This book is printed on paper suitable for recycling and made from fully managed and sustained forest sources.

10 9 8 7 6 5 4 3 2 1
09 08 07 06 05 04 03 02 01 00

Printed and bound in Great Britain by
Antony Rowe Ltd, Chippenham, Wiltshire

Contents

Foreword

Following the international debt crisis of early 1980s, a large number of developing countries adopted various liberalisation and structural programmes. Such programmes attracted large flows of capital into those countries, and created a false image of credibility for the reform programmes. Within a short period of time, the limitations of those economies in absorbing such flows of fund became evident, and the countries witnessed rapid outflows of funds and a serious financial crisis. The first country to face the above experience was Mexico, which in 1994 was hit with the peso crisis. Despite the initial 'Tequila effect', neither the investors, nor the authorities of emerging markets, took much notice of the vulnerability of their economy and financial system, and foreign capital continued to flow into those economies. The next crisis in South East Asia, however, hit the world much more severely and forced everybody to reconsider the problem more critically. The present book provides a critical review of the nature and validity of the reform programmes that have been pursued by some of the emerging markets, and the shortcomings of the rescue packages that have been adopted in the aftermath of the crisis. The idea of publishing this volume was formed in spring 1998 during a conference in Mexico, which was organised by Professor Celso Garrido and was attended by the contributors of the book.

I would like to thank the British Council in Mexico which sponsored the programme of academic link between the University of Westminster and Universidad Autonomo Metropolitan. My thanks also go to my husband Vahab Samadian, who provided invaluable help and support in writing some of the chapters and preparing this volume.

SIMA MOTAMEN-SAMADIAN

Notes on the Contributors

George Croft is Senior Lecturer in Quantitative Methods at the Westminster Business School, University of Westminster, UK.

Celso Garrido is Professor of Finance at the Universidad Autonoma Metropolitana, Mexico.

Akira Kohsaka is Professor of Economics at the Osaka School of International Public Policy, Osaka University, Japan.

Jan A. Kregel is Professor of Economics at the University of Bologna, Italy.

Sima Motamen-Samadian is Senior Lecturer in Economics and Finance at the Westminster Business School, University of Westminster, UK.

Etelberto Ortiz C. is Professor of Economics at the Universidad Autónoma Metropolitana, Mexico.

Ajit Singh is Professor of Economics at the University of Cambridge, UK.

1 Introduction

Sima Motamen-Samadian

During the last two decades, the world economy has been characterised by rapid globalisation of financial markets, and growing integration of capital markets. To fit in to the above framework, the majority of emerging markets implemented various structural and liberalisation programmes, which in the late 1980s and early 1990s attracted many international investors to those economies. In the late 1990s, however, the observers became increasingly concerned about the merits of investment in those markets, both with regards to the economy of the host countries, and with regards to the position of investors and their respective economies. That is because within a short span of time, the world economy witnessed four serious financial crises in emerging markets. The first one was the 1994 Mexican peso crisis, the second one was the 1997 South East Asian crisis, the third one was the 1998 Russian crisis and the fourth was the 1998 Brazilian crisis.

The above crises not only inflicted serious damage on the local and regional economies of the countries concerned but have also adversely affected the prospect of economic growth and stability in the rest of the world. The repeated manner in which they have occurred has raised a number of questions regarding the sources and the management of the problems, and the ability of international financial markets to cope with the spill over effects of such crises. In assessing the causes and consequences of these crises, various authors put their emphasis on different factors. Some have blamed the integration of international capital markets and large flows of capital across countries as the main incipients of the crises. Others highlighted the vulnerability and fragility of the financial systems of emerging markets, and the inappropriate macroeconomic policies that have been adopted by the governments of those economies as the most important contributing factors. Some blamed the process and order of liberalisation, and the nature and format of financial reforms as the causes of the crises. And finally, some criticised the inappropriate methods of crisis management in the aftermath of a crisis, as a cause for concern, and the need for careful reconsideration to avoid future problems.

To have a good understanding of the reasons for the emergence of a crisis, one has to examine the macroeconomic background of the countries involved, and the role of both internal and external factors that contributed to the crisis. Such analysis, though is necessary for a better understanding of the sources of problems, may not be sufficient for prevention of other forthcoming crises, as it is equally important to assess the viability of the policies that have been adopted following a crisis. In other words, it is crucially important to examine the credibility of the so-called 'Crisis Management' policies in each case.

These are some of the main issues that will be addressed in this book. Chapters 2–4 provide an overview of the characteristics of the Mexican economy, which was the first emerging market that experienced a financial crisis. In this respect in Chapter 2 Sima Motamen-Samadian examines the causes and consequences of the Mexican banking crisis, and raises concerns about the question of moral hazard in the format of rescue packages that were introduced in Mexico in the aftermath of the crisis. In Chapter 3 Etelberto Ortiz C. looks at the background to the crisis, and questions the design of the structural reform programme that was pursued in Mexico and highlights its weaknesses. In Chapter 4, Celso Garrido provides a discussion of the strategic response of Mexican enterprises to structural change in that country.

Chapter 5 then moves to South East Asia where the second major crisis of the 1990s occurred. In that chapter, Akira Khosaka offers an assessment of macroeconomic management in the Asia–Pacific region, and its role in the crisis. He identifies the inflexible exchange rates, domestic financial liberalisation and increased access to the international capital market as contributing factors. He then goes on to argue that both the degree and the scope of contagious results, the so-called 'Tom-Yam Effect', are larger than the incipient macroeconomic imbalances. He also identifies the pitfalls of macroeconomic management during the pre-crisis period, and comments on the subsequent crisis management and the global systematic risk management. In his analysis, Khosaka emphasises the importance of the separation of short-term rehabilitation programmes for crisis management and structural reforms. Finally, he argues that the Pacific Asian crisis not only exposed the vulnerability of financial systems in emerging markets but also that of the international financial system and he calls for restructuring of the latter.

Chapter 6 opens up a debate on the future prospect of an emerging market that is still thriving, namely, India. Ajit Singh reviews the characteristics of the Indian stock market, and the reform programmes that have been implemented in the process of development of that market. He then goes on to highlight the type of problems that India may face in the future if due attention is not paid to the pattern of corporate control in that country.

In Chapter 7, Jan A. Kregel draws attentions to the importance of prudential regulation and the need for a new approach to the question of reform of financial systems in developing countries. In his discussion, he argues that the problem of reform should not be reduced to whether bank-based development is more appropriate or market-based reform, as both are required to provide liquidity. The question, Kregel argues, should be that of how to provide an appropriate programme of reform to ensure the development of a prudential system. In his analysis, Kregel highlights the weak points of both market-based and bank-based financial structures in both developed and developing countries, and concludes that prudential regulation should be extended across borders to enhance the flow of capital.

Finally, in Chapter 8, Sima Motamen-Samadian and George Croft focus on the role of capital flows in the stability of foreign exchange markets, and ask why, while large flows of funds across developed markets do not necessarily destabilise those markets, the same flows are likely to cause a crisis in emerging markets. In examining the above question, they present a theoretical model of emerging markets that shows the conditions under which a change in the size of capital flows may alter the stability of a market. The model is rather similar to other portfolio balance models, but incorporates some of the specific features of emerging markets.

2 Mexican banking crisis: causes and consequences

Sima Motamen-Samadian

Following the sharp devaluation of the peso at the end of 1994, and the ensuing financial crisis, the Mexican economy went through a deep recession in 1995. To restore macroeconomic stability, and control the rapidly rising inflation, the government adopted a number of drastic stabilisation measures, which though extremely painful, appeared to deliver some positive results. By the year end 1996, the rate of inflation measured by the consumer price index, was reduced to 27.7 per cent, which was almost one half of its peak of 52 per cent in 1995, and the real GDP which had declined by 6.2 per cent in 1995, showed a positive growth of 5.1 per cent. In this respect, the growth of exports and foreign direct investments, which were stimulated by the depreciation of the Peso and engagement of NAFTA, played a very important role. During 1996, foreign direct investments, which entered the country, amounted to $7.6 billion of which $4.6 billion corresponded to new investments, and $3 billion was related to reinvestment of earnings and inter-company accounts. In terms of country of origin, 74.8 per cent of the new investments came for the NAFTA members (65.9 per cent from the US and 8.9 per cent from Canada). The most important recipients of the foreign investments were the industrial and the services sector, which received 57.1 and 25.8 per cent of the new investments respectively. The remaining recipients were commerce (8.7 per cent), transportation and communications (6.3 per cent), and other sectors (2.1 per cent).

The above results suggest that the combination of the stabilisation programmes and financial rescue packages that were introduced in 1995 were effective to some extent in stabilising the exchange rate, reducing inflation and restoring economic activity.

During 1996, the slow recovery of the economy and the ability of the government to reduce inflation, enabled the Mexican public sector (including development banks) to return to the international capital markets, and carry out a number of successful placements of medium-term bonds and promissory notes. The resources thus obtained helped the government to prepay the whole of the financial assistance funds that they had received from the US treasury, and about one-third of the SDR credit that they had obtained from the IMF. The above fund raising also helped to make early payments on expensive liabilities and improve the maturity profile of public sector external debt.

Nevertheless, despite the above achievements, Mexican banks continue to struggle with the after shocks of the crisis, and have a long way to go before full recovery. The banking sector was in fact the sector, that was most severely affected by the downturn in economic activities and the contraction of domestic demand in 1995. To prevent a widespread bank failure and restore the public's confidence in the banking system, the government introduced a number of financial support programmes that averted the total collapse of the banking industry. As a result, even though a number of banks were sold to foreign interests, no banks were liquidated.

The support programmes though crucial in rescuing the banking industry have been implemented at a very high cost. According to the Bank of Mexico's report, *The Mexican Economy 1997*, by the end of 1996, the total cost of government financial support programmes to the banks amounted to 210.3 billion pesos, which was about 8.4 per cent of GDP. Private estimates, however, put the above figure at a higher level. One of the important issues, however, that may not be fully apparent as yet, is the extent by which the events of the last few years have contributed to the spread of moral hazard.

The present chapter attempts to highlight some of the structural changes which took place in the banking industry in the 1990s, and the specific factors which contributed to the liquidity crunch of the banking sector after the 1994 peso crisis. It will also discuss the nature of the financial assistance packages that were adopted by the government to assist the banking sector and the role of NAFTA in that. Moreover, it will assess the implications of the new policies regarding the future practice of banks and the effectiveness of the support programmes in averting banking crises. Finally there will be some concluding remarks regarding the future of the Mexican banking sector.

BANKING REFORMS PRIOR TO THE 1994 CRISIS

In the early 1990s, the Mexican government adopted a number of measures to liberalise the financial sector. Among the reform programmes, two measures were considered very important, namely the privatisation of banks which started in May 1990 and ended in June 1992, and the relaxation of capital control in November 1991, which was accompanied by a quasi fixed exchange rate regime in the form of an upper band on the peso exchange rate *vis-à-vis* dollar. The above reforms were not only considered essential in terms of increasing the availability of funds for investment purposes but were also particularly important in view of the future integration of Mexico in to NAFTA in 1992, and the global integration into the international financial capital markets. The outcome of the reform programmes, however, revealed that the privatisation of banks did not exactly lead to greater efficiency and competition among the financial intermediaries. Rather, it contributed to a greater concentration of capital among certain financial groups in the financial system, and an oligopolistic structure in the banking industry.

The main objectives of the privatization were: (a) to reduce the public sector deficit; (b) to improve the availability of funds to private firms and convince the business community about the government's commitment to restructure the Mexican economy; and (c) to assure depositors about the sound operation of financial markets, and correct management of their funds.

In view of the forthcoming NAFTA at that time it was important for the government to show a determination in reducing its internal and external public debt. In 1990, even though the ratio of total public sector debt to GDP appeared to have fallen from 61.9 per cent in 1988 to 45.8 per cent in 1990, and the external debt accounted for 28.5 per cent of GDP, the above ratios were considered to be too high and in need of adjustment. In that respect, bank privatisation not only would have enabled the government to reduce their total debt but also would have helped them to direct the proceeds to targeted social spending.

It was also important to enhance the confidence of the private sector in the efficiency of the financial sector. By the late 1980s and early 1990s, the existing nationalized banks[1] were beginning to show signs of inefficiency. As Elizondo (1993) points out, banks were losing ground *vis-à-vis* other financial institutions, and corruption was starting to appear. This became more apparent when, after the privatisation in 1992, the new bank owners discovered that poor allocation of credit prior to the privatisation had created much higher past-due loans than were expected. It is also important to note that bank savings in Mexico is highly concentrated among a very small number of individuals and firms, who make up a very large proportion of total deposit liabilities of banks. According to the 1992 Bank of Mexico's report, in 1991 accounts of more than 96,000 individuals and firms with 250 million pesos or more, made up only 0.37 per cent of total bank accounts, and in total amounted to 66.10[2] per cent of total bank deposits. Thus, it was very important to assure the business community of the soundness of financial sector.

Prior to the privatisation, there were rumours that due to closeness of government officials with the bidders, there was a possibility that banks may be sold below their actual value. It was also considered possible that the bidders may attempt to reward the officials in the form of favourable credits after the bank privatisation for accepting low bids. As far as the government was concerned, however, the prime objective was to maximise the revenue from privatisation. Moreover, it was very important for the government to show that the process of privatisation was not biased in favour of the bidders and against the public's interest.

Therefore, in order to avoid any possibility of mismanagement and rumour of collusion between the officials and the bidders, the government set up a committee to oversee the process of privatisation. The committee conducted the process of share distribution in two stages. In the first round, it was responsible: (a) to determine the value of banks that were going to be privatised with the aid of external audit, and (b) to ensure the sound economic position and moral credibility of the bidders. Thus, during the first round, the bidders were aware of the identity of the other bidders. In the second round, the committee had to allocate the banks according to the highest bids in a secret auction.

In total, even though only 44 groups bid for the 18 nationalised banks, the government managed to sell the banks at very high prices. The government was expecting to receive between 24 and 30 billion new pesos. By the end of the privatisation, however, they managed to obtain 60 billion new pesos of which 29.9 billion pesos was received in 1991 and 30.1 billion pesos in 1992. The proceeds in 1991 amounted to 3.2 per cent of GDP, and in 1992 to 2.7 per cent of GDP. In total the amount received from privatisation was nearly three times what they had expected. According to official figures, on average banks were sold at 3.07 times their book value, and 14.07 times their profit. In total, bank shares were distributed among only 130,000 people, which was a very low number for such an important industry. Most of the new shareholders were in effect the biggest depositors who after the privatisation became the part owners of banks, and directly or indirectly took over the management of their savings.

Following the privatisation the budgetary balance of the public sector improved from –0.4 per cent of GDP in 1991 to 1.4 per cent in 1992.[3] The proceed also helped to reduce the public sector debt from 339.6 billion pesos in 1991 to 300.7 billion pesos in 1992, and 274.6 billion pesos in 1993. Following the privatisation, the public sectors' domestic debt declined from 131.3 billion new pesos in 1991 to 89.7 billion new pesos in 1992, and 54.4 billion new pesos in 1994. Over the same period, as indicated in the 1997 Bank of Mexico report, total public sector debt as a proportion of GDP declined from 35.8 per cent in 1991 to 21.9 per cent in 1994.

As far as the bidders were concerned, the high prices paid for banks were justified by the specific position of banks in the Mexican financial system. At the time of privatisation the financial sector in Mexico was rather underdeveloped and the bank finance was one of the important sources of finance for the corporate sector. Moreover, the banking industry was a highly protected industry, and the profitability of Mexican banks was about three times higher than their US and Canadian counterparts. Furthermore, despite, all the moves towards openness in relation to the NAFTA, the banking industry after the privatisation remained one of the most protected industries. That was because the government was determined to keep the banks under Mexican control. So, even though the US banks were counting on NAFTA to play a role in opening of Mexican financial system to greater foreign competition, and enable them to create their own branches in Mexico, the NAFTA negotiations only led to the approval of opening of subsidiaries. Moreover, the new banking law set the maximum limit for foreign investment in a Mexican bank at 30 per cent of the bank's capital, and a limit of 1.5 per cent of the total market share for any individual subsidiary of a foreign bank. The new regulation also assured Mexican banks that they could benefit from a temporary protection during the next four years after the privatisation if the overall foreigners' control increased beyond 25 per cent of the market. Therefore, in view of the economic growth prospects associated with NAFTA and the above projectionist measures, the bidders of banks were confident that in the absence of serious foreign competition, Mexican banks were going to grow even further in the future. Thus, in effect as argued by both Elizondo (1993) and Perrotini (1996), the bidders were paying the high prices for the right to own a bank rather than the actual value of the banks. In addition to the above protectionist environment, the new bankers were going to face a less regulated environment, where quantitative credit controls were to disappear, compulsory reserve requirements were going to be abolished, and fixing of interest rates no longer prevailed. This implied that the high prices paid by the new bankers included some hidden profits, which could materialise in real terms after the privatisation.

One of the important features of the new banking structure was the establishment of the new financial groups, which was a move towards the establishment of the system of universal banking. The new regulations, while prohibiting industrial or commercial firms from the ownership of banks, allowed banks to own up to a maximum of 5 per cent of the total shares of firms that were not related to banking. On the other hand, according to the new regulations, bank ownership was restricted to only individuals and financial groups. Moreover, the ownership of either an individual or a financial group was restricted to a maximum of 5 per cent of the total bank shares. This was more restrictive than the bank regulations before the nationalisation of 1982, when one individual or a firm could own and control a bank. Thus, in terms of ownership, though the new regulations appeared to be more restrictive with respect to maximum ownership of capital and firm ownership of banks, they opened the possibility of ownership to financial groups who in turn were allowed to own firms.

Here, it is important to note that as Elizondo (1993) points out the ownership of industrial groups in Mexico is highly concentrated and one family or even an individual can own more than 50 per cent of the shares of a business group. Therefore, it was not difficult for an individual to assemble a group of investors related to a certain business group to get together and invest in a bank. Moreover, the financial groups such as brokerage houses, credit-card companies, and insurance companies were in a much better position to secure funds externally and bid for the banks. That is why only those groups that could raise higher amounts of funds from external sources participated in bidding for banks. Moreover, even though the financial groups could bid for only 5 per cent of a banks' capital, in practice they managed to take over the management of some very important banks. For example, Eugenio Garza Laguera who was the former owner of Serfin before the nationalisation of 1982, and controlled Visa after the nationalisation in 1982, took over the control of Bancomer, which was the second biggest bank after the privatisation. Adrian Sada, the owner of Vitro (a credit-card company), who also had acquired the Anchor Glass Containers Corporation, and controlled a powerful brokerage house, took over the control of Serfin, which is the third biggest bank in Mexico. Augustin Legorreta, who controlled the second biggest brokerage house, took over the control of Comermex, which is the fourth biggest bank.

It is also important to point out that some of the private financiers managed to retain only the controlling shares, and through financial engineering secured the banks without actually investing all the capital that was initially going to be paid for the banks. Moreover, despite the regulatory restriction on the maximum amount of shares that an individual could hold, in practice some individuals managed to reinforce their control over several banks by putting themselves on the boards of a number of banks and thus enjoyed a powerful position.

The new regulation, appeared to be rather restrictive in terms of the amount of credits that a bank could extend to its owners. Under the new regulation, the maximum amount of credits that a bank could extend to the firms owned by the banks or by the members of the board or principle shareholders was set at 20 per cent of total bank credits. Moreover, the credits had to be approved by two-thirds of the members of the board of shareholders type 'A' (51 per cent of total shares) and 60 per cent of board members representing type 'B' and 'C' (shares open to foreigners). One important advantage of these loans was that the above borrowers could acquire the credit at below market rate. Moreover, the higher the level of a bank's total credit extended, the higher would have been the absolute value of that 20 per cent of total credit that a bank was allowed to extend to an individual shareholder, or a member of the board or firm owned by the bank. Hence, in order to be able to get a higher amount of cheap credit, the board members had a vested interest in allowing the banks to increase credit to borrowers, beyond an acceptable level compatible with capital adequacy margin.

Overall, privatisation of the banking sector in Mexico although it helped the government to reduce the public debt it did not exactly lead to greater competition and openness of the market. In this respect, NAFTA played an important role in enhancing the process of privatisation, and the success of the government in selling the shares of privatised banks at high prices. But it did not play a significant role in opening the banking industry to greater foreign competition and improving their efficiency. The main outcome of the privatisation was the change in the structure of the banking industry from a state monopoly to a private oligopoly.

PERFORMANCE OF BANKS AFTER THE PRIVATISATION

Financial reforms in Mexico were introduced at the time when the economic recession in the US and other industrialised countries had pushed the US and other international interest rates below the Mexican level. The above developments had two serious and far-reaching implications regarding the position of financial markets. First, they opened a window of opportunity for the newly privatised banks to borrow at a cheaper rate from the international markets and use the funds for lending at a higher rate in the domestic markets. Secondly, they led to a considerable rise in short-term capital inflow, and hence a real appreciation of the exchange rates, which was not exactly justified by the macroeconomic fundamentals of the country. Indeed, the real appreciation of the peso which followed, misguided both domestic financial and non-financial private sector and foreign agents about the real strength of the peso and the ability of the private sector to borrow both from the domestic and the international markets. As later events showed, the above false belief, which proved to be disastrously wrong, seriously undermined the position of the Mexican banks in 1995.

Between 1992 to 1994, the external debt of both commercial banks and the non-bank private sector increased by 34.22, and 62.57 per cent respectively (see Table 2.1).

Table 2.1 Total external debt (billions of US$)

Year	*1990*	*1991*	*1992*	*1993*	*1994*	*Rate of growth (%), 1992–94*	*1995*	*1996*
Total external debt	104.3	116.5	117.5	131.7	142.2	21.02	169.9	164.9
Public sector	77.8	80.0	75.8	78.7	85.4	12.66	100.9	98.3
Commercial banks	12.2	17.8	18.7	23.8	25.1	34.22	20.9	19.4
Bank of Mexico	6.5	6.8	6.0	4.8	3.9	–35	17.3*	13.3
Private non-bank sector	7.8	12.0	17.1	24.4	27.8	62.57	30.7	34.0

* Includes $1.5 billion corresponding to the North-American Framework Agreement (NAFA) signed with the financial authorities from the US and Canada.

Source: Bank of Mexico (1997), *The Mexican Economy 1997.*

Under the new regulatory environment, with no compulsory reserve requirement, and no fixed interest rates, the newly privatised banks were actively involved in granting credit to the private sector. This is evident from Table 2.2, which shows that within two years after the privatisation, the amount of financing granted by banks to the private sector increased by nearly 40 per cent. In 1994, commercial banks' financing to the private sector reached nearly 44 per cent of GDP.

The new owners thus managed to pass on the high cost of buying the banks to consumers through a rise in the level of loans to the private and public sector, higher margins between the deposit and loan rates, and higher bank service charges. The combination of the above factors also contributed to a rise in banks' profits. In 1992, the profits of 12 banks, including the 3 biggest banks were 35 per cent higher in real terms than in the previous year. For example Banamax, the biggest bank increased its profits by 45 per cent.

Immediately after the privatisation, share prices of listed banks sharply increased, and in some cases, they rose by more than 15 per cent in the same day. Thus, a number of new shareholders of the banks managed to sell their shares with high profits. But the stock market remained unconvinced about the future profits of the banks, and within a short period of time after the privatisation, share prices of most banks dropped. That was mainly because in 1993 and 1994 the

Table 2.2 Financing granted by consolidated banks in both domestic and foreign currency (billions of new pesos)

Year	*1991*	*1992*	*1993*	*1994**	*Rate of growth (%), 1992–94*	*1995*	*1996*
Total	430.2	526.1	600.3	683.2	29.9		
Public sector	160.1	126.2	93.3	122.8	−2.7	100.9	98.3
Financial	13.1	16.3	23.1	40.0	145.4	n.a.	n.a.
Non-financial	146.9	109.9	70.1	82.8	−24.6	n.a.	n.a.
Private sector	250.0	372.16	470.4	520.6	39.9	763.9	863.1
Individual**	n.a.	128.59	116.93	135.32	5.2	204.1	242.9
Firms**	n.a.	243.57	353.47	385.28	58.2	559.8	620.2

* The figure for 1994 corresponds to May 1994.
** These figures were calculated by the author for the years 1992–94.
Source: INEGI (1994) *Mexican Bulletin of Statistical Information*, no. 13, July–Sept. and no. 26, October–December 1997 (INEGI, Instituto Nacional de Estadistica Geografia e Informatica); and Bank of Mexico (1997) *The Mexican Economy 1997*.

rapid increase in loans to the private sector had started to show signs of strain in the private sector. According to the Bank of Mexico's report, *The Mexican Economy 1995*, the ratio of past-due loans to total loan portfolio of commercial banks increased from 7.1 per cent in December 1993 to 8.2 per cent in December 1994. Among the component of past-due loan portfolio of commercial banks, overdue principal showed the highest rate of growth. Between December 1992 and December 1993, the above items grew by 5.5 per cent and between December 1993 and December 1994, they grew by 6.5 per cent. The loans that were granted for the purchase of durable consumer goods, credit cards, and agricultural and livestock projects, made the highest ratio of past due loans to total loan portfolio and in December 1994 registered at 26.8, 13.3 and 10.5 per cent respectively.

The growth in past-due loan portfolios in 1994 was also evident among leasing and financial factoring companies. As reported by the Bank of Mexico in 1995, the ratio of past-due loan portfolio for leasing companies increased from 9.4 per cent in 1993 to 10.3 per cent in 1994. Over the same period, the same ratio in the case of factoring companies, rose from 8.4 to 13.2 per cent. The above data indicates that the financial groups who were part owners of banks were also beginning to experience difficulties.

Generally, the objective of creating a universal banking system is to improve the allocative efficiency of markets. Under a universal banking system, banks are supposed to be able to monitor the operation of the borrowers more closely, and thus reduce the risks of loan defaults due to asymmetric information. This should help banks not to ration credit according to the expected value of loan return. This is believed to be crucial in enhancing the channelling of funds in a more efficient manner.

In the case of Mexico, however, the above type of universal banking generated the opposite outcome. In the sense that the management of the financial groups, who were also the stockholders of both banks and some of the industries, had vested interest in encouraging bank managers to approve the granting of loans to their respective firms. In doing so, they were not necessarily concerned about the interests of depositors, or exposure of banks to bad debt, but in securing credit for their own firms.[4] In this way, the universal banking turned out to serve the opposite purpose of its initial objective in Mexico. In practice, whereas the amount of credits to private individuals and firms increased, the provisions of reserves against bad debt did not rise in line. Nor did the risk adjusted capitalisation margins. This became apparent in 1994, when despite the apparent efforts of commercial banks to create additional preventive reserves to write off irrevocable loans, the ratio of preventive reserves to total past-due loan portfolio decreased from 44.6 per cent in 1993 to 42.1 per cent in 1994. The inadequacy of the above ratios is more apparent when compared with the 60 per cent compulsory cautionary reserve ratio to past-due loans that was imposed in 1995.

In September 1994, the evidence of irregularities in the operations of two banks, Union and Cremi compelled the National Banking and Securities Commission to intervene in the management of those banks. The interventions involved granting of financial support via the Bank Fund for the Protection of Savings (FOBAPROA[5]).

ECONOMIC PROBLEMS OF 1994 PESO CRISIS AND FINANCIAL ASSISTANCE AFTER THE CRISIS

The peso crisis of 1994 created two very immediate problems for Mexico. First, it posed a very serious problem for the authorities as far as the short-term external debts denominated in foreign currency were concerned, and secondly, it pushed the Mexican economy in to a deep recession and the banking system to the brink of collapse.

As far as the foreign debt was concerned, one of the immediate problems of the Mexican government was the obligation to meet $29 billion short-term debt in the form of Tesobonos (short-term treasury bills denominated in dollars), which was maturing in 1995. At the end of 1994, as reported by the Bank of Mexico in 1995, Mexico's total external debt amounted to $142.6 billion. This was at the time when the international reserves, which had fallen to just over $11 billion, were insufficient to meet the demand of agents for conversion of pesos to dollars, and the collapse of international investors' confidence in Mexican economy had made it impossible for the Mexican authorities to roll-over short-term debt.

On the other hand, as far as the domestic economy was concerned, the crisis created the following problems for the banks. First, the sharp depreciation of the peso, and the rise in US interest rates increased the debt burden of banks, and reduced their ability to help the domestic market.[6] Secondly, the depreciation of currency had increased the debt burden of the private non-bank sector, and in turn adversely affected their ability to repay their loans to domestic banks.[7] Thirdly, the tight monetary policy, which was pursued to control inflation, had resulted in a sharp rise in interest rate, which in turn significantly increased the size of domestic debt burden and reduced the ability of domestic borrowers to repay their debt. In 1995, inflation measured by consumer prices and producer prices increased to a high level of 52 and 59.5 per cent respectively, and the average interbank interest rate rose to 54.05 per cent, compared with 17.84 per cent in the previous year. Fourthly, the contraction of demand caused by the high level of interest rates also affected the ability of domestic businesses to repay their debt.

During 1995, the sharp fall in gross fixed capital formation and private consumption, which dropped by 29 per cent and 9.5 per cent respectively, resulted in a fall in real GDP which declined by 6.2 per cent. The sharp fall in economic activities also resulted in a rise in the rate of unemployment, which increased by 8.6[8] per cent between 1994 to 1995.

The combination of all the above factors resulted in a large number of loan defaults. To the extent that in August 1995, the ratio of past-due loans to total loans of commercial banks peaked to the high level of 12.1 per cent, which was nearly four times higher than the ceiling suggested by the Basle Accord. Thus, many banks were threatened by the possibility of insolvency.

Therefore, to overcome the short-term liquidity crisis in both the foreign and domestic front, the Mexican authorities were forced to take two sets of urgent actions. First, to manage the external crisis, the Mexican government appealed to the international community for financial assistance, and secondly to abort domestic crisis they engaged in providing financial assistance to the domestic banking sector.

FOREIGN ASSISTANCE

In terms of foreign financial assistance, NAFTA membership proved to be very useful for Mexico. In early 1995, the Mexican government managed to negotiate a total of $51.6 billion multilateral financial assistance package with the IMF, United States, the Bank of Canada, the BIS, the World Bank, and the Inter-American Development Bank. The above figure included $20 billion which was pledged by the United States in loans and security guarantees from the Exchange Stabilization Fund (ESF), approximately $1.1 billion pledged by the Bank of Canada under the North American Framework Agreement (NAFA),[9] $17.8 billion Stand-by arrangement offered by the IMF, $10 billion credit line offered by the BIS, and $2.8 billion in credit by the World Bank and the Inter-American Development Bank.

The Stand-by arrangement, which was made with the IMF in late January 1995, was initially for 18 months and allowed Mexico to draw up to a limit of 12.1 billion SDR (approximately $17.8 billion). Mexico, however, made only four drawings during 1995 for a total of SDR 8.8 billion (approximately $9.2 billion). The resources obtained from the IMF were mainly used to clear part of the dollar-denominated public securities, which were maturing during 1995, and to strengthen the international reserves of the Bank of Mexico. In mid-July 1996, Mexico requested another six-month extension on the Stand-by agreement with the IMF, in order to maintain a precautionary credit line. On that occasion, although the IMF approved Mexico's request in August 1996, Mexico did not actually make any drawings.

Of the $20 billion pledged by the United States in February 1995, the Federal Reserves agreed to provide up to $6 billion in short-term swaps under NAFA, and the Treasury Department agreed to provide backing for the Federal Reserve swaps by assuring repayment on any short-term drawings against the $20 billion limit. In practice, the Mexican authorities used only $13.5 billion of the total amount pledged. In accordance with the Agreements signed with the US government on February 1995, most of the funds were used to redeem Tesobonos and other short-term dollar denominated debt of the Mexican government and its agencies. As will be discussed later, by early 1997, Mexico managed to prepay and clear all the loans it had received from the US.

In the case of $1.1 billion pledged by the Bank of Canada, Mexico used only $355 million, and repaid it in full by the end of 1996.

Finally the $10 billion credit line that was offered by the BIS was not used.

DOMESTIC FINANCIAL ASSISTANCE TO BANKS AND DEBTORS

To prevent the possibility of a widespread bank failure, the Mexican government arranged a number of rescue packages to assist both the debtors who could not repay their loans, and the banks which were in danger of insolvency.

The programmes in support of debtors, although devised to provide assistance for a limited period, had the following objectives in mind:

(a) to promote responsible payment practices and encourage borrowers to keep up with their debt repayment, (b) to encourage banks to provide additional credit to credible debtors who were covered by the programmes, and (c) to support small debtors. The costs of the programmes were to be shared by both the banks and the Federal Government. In addition, as the programmes were not injecting any money into the system, they did not have any monetary impact.

Programmes to assist debtors

The programmes to assist debtors included five packages, namely:

- Restructuring of Loans in Investment Units (UDIs[10])
- Additional Benefits Programme for Mortgage Loan Debtors
- Immediate Support Programme for Debtors (ADE[11])
- Agricultural, Livestock and Fisheries Loan Support Programme (FINAPE[12])
- Support Programme for Small and Medium-sized Firms (FOPYME[13])

The above packages were designed to address the needs of five groups of debtors, and help them to continue repaying their loans. Let us now consider each programme in more detail.

Restructuring of loans in investment units (UDIs)

The first programme briefly referred to as the UDI programme addressed the need of those debtors who held intrinsically viable loans, but had difficulty in servicing their debt due to volatility of inflation and nominal interest rate. This programme was introduced in April 1995, with the objective of converting large number of loans into units of investment called UDIs and transferring them to trust funds, which were set up for that purpose in exchange for special CETES issued by the government. An UDI is an inflation-indexed unit of account, which is fixed, in real terms with daily adjustment to inflation rate. With conversion of loans into UDIs, loan maturity is lengthened, and by inflation refinancing, the immediate liquidity pressures on borrowers are alleviated. The government lends banks the funds to finance restructured loans at a real interest rate. The above loans are denominated in UDIs. In return, the government borrows from banks, by placing government instruments at market rates. When the debtors repay their loan, the proceeds will be used to amortise the government's funding. Thus, while the borrowers are charged a fixed real interest rate, the government bears the risk of mismatch in interest rates if the interest collected on its lending to banks in UDIs is lower than the real interest rate it has to pay on its own debt instruments, and the banks continue to carry the credit and funding risks. At the end of 1995, the programme was expanded to allow for restructuring of foreign currency loans.

By the end of 1996, 166.9 billion pesos of bank loans were restructured though the UDI programme, of which 58.69 per cent were related to mortgage loans, 30.6 per cent corresponded to loans to productive plants, 10.59 per cent were commercial banks' loans to public sector, and the remaining 0.12 per cent were other restructured loans. In total, over 258 billion pesos of banks loans were restructured of which 64.57 per cent were restructured through UDI programme, and the remaining 35.43 per cent through banks' own programme. The fiscal cost of UDIs programme for the government was 21.6 billion pesos.

Additional benefits programme for mortgage loan debtors

Initially, the debtors whose mortgage loan were restructured were those who had acquired a mortgage loans of up to 57,700 million pesos. In early 1996, however, the government realised that despite the earlier restructuring, a very large number of borrowers continued to have very little or no incentive to keep up with their mortgage repayments. That was because: (a) despite the restructuring of their loans in UDIs, the monthly repayments continued to absorb a very proportion of their income and exerted a very heavy burden on them, and (b) the weak real estate market had reduced the value of their properties below the outstanding principal of the corresponding UDI-denominated loan. Therefore, in May 1996, the government expanded the programme to cover mortgages of up to 135,521 million pesos that were restructured prior to April 1996.

The supplementary programme enabled the borrowers to receive a discount on their payments for ten years. The discounts, which applied only to the first 500,000, UDIs, started at 30 per cent for payments in 1996, and progressively declined to 5 per cent over the next 10 years of payments. To further encourage the borrowers to repay their mortgages, an additional discount of 10 per cent was offered to those who were prepared to make early payments and clear their loans before 31 May 1999. Moreover, in order to reactivate the real estate market, additional discounts were provided to those who had made contracts for the construction of houses, which were either finished or were still under construction. Overall, by the end of 1996, 84.3 per cent of all mortgage loans received support from the programme. The cost of the discounts, which was entirely to be born by the government, amounted to 27.2 billion pesos.

Immediate support programme for debtors (ADE)

The objective of this programme was to help various groups of debtors with an immediate debt repayment problem to return to current standing. It was also aimed at promoting the loan restructuring. The support provided under the ADE package, was a one-year interest rate subsidy to all those borrowers who had contracted various loans such as consumer, credit card, personal, mortgage, small business and agricultural loans in terms of either domestic currency or in UDI prior to August 1995.

The package also provided non-monetary supports in the form of temporarily halting foreclosure proceedings against defaulting debtors and standardisation of restructuring procedures. By the end of 1996, according to the Bank of Mexico 1997 report, nearly 2 million loan contracts with a value of over 250 billion pesos were restructured. The fiscal cost of ADEs for the government was 4.3 billion pesos.

Agricultural, livestock and fisheries loan support programme (FINAP[14])

This programme addressed the need of bank debtors from the agricultural, livestock and fisheries sectors. Similar to the Mortgage programme, the FINAPE provided payment discounts for a period of maximum ten years. The size of discounts varied for different size of loans, but was fixed for the entire period it was granted. The maximum discount was 40 per cent for loans up to 500,000 pesos, and the lowest discount was 16 per cent for loans of between 2 to 4 million pesos. The costs of these discounts were to be shared between the Federal Government and the banks. The fiscal costs of these discounts for the government amounted to 14.2 billion pesos.

Support programme for small and medium-sized firms (FOPYME[15])

This programme provided discount support for small business loans of up to 6 million pesos, denominated in domestic currency, UDI or US dollars. Here again, the discounts, which varied between 30 to 17 per cent, were granted for a period of 10 years on the basis of amount of each loan. The package provided support to those debtors who were either up to date with their debt repayment, or in arrears but returning to current position, and those who had restructured their loans before 31 January 1997. The costs of this package is also going to be shared between the banks and the Federal Government, with the government bearing the larger proportion of the costs, the greater the amount of fresh financing granted by banks. The fiscal costs of this package for the government have been estimated to be 7.4 billion pesos.

No doubt, at the time of a deep recession it is very important for a government to act promptly by easing the burden of debt repayment for the borrowers, and helping the banks with large problem loans to stay afloat. In this respect, the packages introduced by the Mexican authorities were helpful in promoting the culture of debt repayment. However, the acceptance of the very high costs of the programme by the government without acquiring any ownership right, while imposing a heavy burden on public and future generation, relieves the banks of the responsibility of bearing the entire costs of their earlier poor practice. It is in this respect that the design of package raises a question of moral hazard. Once the private owners of banks know that if they are in acute difficulty, the government comes to their rescue without acquiring part ownership of banks, they may repeat the same practice in future without fearing the full financial consequences of their poor practice.

Apart from the above packages, which were designed to help debtors, the government also introduced a number of support packages to strengthen the position of banks in difficulty.

The programmes to strengthen banks

In January 1995, the Mexican government introduced several measures to ease the pressure on the banking system. The government considered it important to provide enough support to enable large and solid institutions to remain in business and preserve depositors' confidence in the banking system, particularly considering the fact that the banks with the most acute bad debt problems were the largest banks (see Gonzalez-Hermosillo *et al.*, 1997).

First, a special dollar fund was provided through the Bank of Mexico to help banks repay their short-term foreign debt. After serving a vital role at the beginning of 1995, the above provision was no longer considered necessary in later months and ceased in September 1995. Secondly, to inject capital into the banking system, two packages were launched. These were:

- Temporary capitalisation programme (PROCAPTE[16])
- Permanent capitalisation measures

Temporary capitalisation programme (PROCAPTE)

This programme was put in to place in 24 February 1995. As reported by the Bank of Mexico (1995), the banks which joined PROCAPTE were obliged to place subordinated debentures necessarily convertible into capital stock of the bank that issued them. The debentures were bought by the FOBAPROA, the Saving Protection Fund, with the financing granted by the Bank of Mexico. The proceeds from these placements constituted money deposits in the Bank of Mexico, with the same maturity and yields as those of the debentures issued. The programme was designed to last for a period of 5 years, during which time the institutions joining the programme are obliged to maintain a capital ratio of at least 9 per cent.

The original credits granted under this programme was 7 billion pesos in June 1995, but by the end of 1996, the total outstanding balance amounted to 11.89 billion pesos.

Permanent capitalisation measures

To provide incentives for this programme of bank capitalisation, the government introduced a second programme through FOBAPROA (the Bank Fund for the Protection of Savings). Under this scheme, banks' loan portfolio was sold to FOBAPROA in return for high capitalisation, in that FOBAPROA offered to buy two pesos worth of banks' duly qualified and provisioned loan portfolio for every one peso of fresh capital paid by stockholders. In exchange, banks had to purchase long-term bonds issued by FOBAPROA. By the end of 1996, as a result of this programme, the capital of banks increased by almost 158 per cent compared with the level in December 1994, and the value of portfolios purchased by FOBAPROA, net of provisions, amounted to 119.3 billion pesos.

Additional measures

In addition to the above two packages, in order to further encourage injection of new capital in banking sector, the government amended some of the regulations regarding limits to ownership. First, they eased some of the restrictions on shareholding for both foreign banks and domestic corporations, and raised the maximum limit for foreign investments in Mexican banks from 30 to 49 per cent. Moreover, the limit on individual shareholding in financial groups, commercial banks or brokerage firms was raised to 20 per cent of capital stock. In the case of investments made by foreign financial institutions, the above limit may be raised even further with the Ministry of Finance's authorisation.

Apart from the above packages, the government also introduced a new measure to tighten provision requirements and reinforce supervision. Most importantly, in February 1995, the National Banking and Securities Commission ordered banks to increase the cautionary reserves with either 60 per cent reserves for non-performing loans, or 4 per cent of total loan portfolio. Moreover, in order to improve control of monetary aggregates, in March 1995, the Bank of Mexico introduced a new system of reserve requirements.

Furthermore, to improve the fundamental problems of the financial system, the government introduced a number of new regulatory rules: (a) to improve the supervisory capacity of the National Banking and Securities Commission; (b) to improve the availability of information to investors through the increased participation of external auditors and securities rating agencies; (c) to revise capitalisation ratios to take into account exposure to market risk; and (d) to improve the accounting standards comparable to internationally accepted accounting principles.

Finally, along with the above packages and measures, in March 1996, the Mexican government set up a new agency called Asset Valuation and Sale Agency (VVA[17]) with the main objectives of making a sound assessment of the value of the assets acquired by the FOBAPROA. In doing so, the agency is responsible for: (1) maximizing revenue from the sale of financial assets, real estate and other property acquired by FOBAPROA; (2) selling the assets through a transparent and open process as fast as condition permits; (3) designing formulas to help restructure viable companies so that they may grow again; and (4) helping to develop a market for banks' debt securities.

Overall, five commercial banks with acute capital inadequacy problems were intervened and received credit through PROCAPTE, and 12 banks benefited form the permanent capitalisation programme through FOBAPROA. Of the five banks, which were initially intervened, the deposits and branches of two banks, Banca Cremi/Oriente, and Banca Union was later sold to Banco de Bilbao Vizcaya, and

Banca Promax respectively. Arrangements were also made for the sale of the deposits and branch office network of Banipais, Interestatal, Suerste and Obrero to foreign Canadian and Spanish banks.

In total, as reported by the Bank of Mexico (1997), the net present value estimation of the costs of all the rescue packages was estimated to be approximately 210.3 billion new pesos which was 8.4 per cent of GDP in 1996. The cost of packages will be born over a 30-year period. The packages, though managed to rescue some banks from the possibility of bankruptcy, did not eliminate the entire problem of bad debt. They mostly allowed banks to transfer approximately 40 per cent of the credits with problems to the government.

THE EFFECTIVENESS OF THE RESCUE PACKAGES

The most important effect of the multilateral rescue funds that were made available to Mexico in 1995/96 was that they helped the Mexican government to overcome its short-term liquidity crisis, and to avoid defaulting on its external debt obligations. They also helped the government to concentrate on its domestic stabilisation policies and reduce the rate of inflation. All these helped the Mexican government to return to international capital markets in 1996, and to restructure their loan profile and maturity. During 1996, the Mexican government made 24 placements of medium-term bonds and promissory notes, worth a total of $16.6 billion. The average maturity of the new loans was raised to 7 years, compared with the average of 27 months in 1995. Moreover, the resources thus obtained helped the government to make early payments on expensive liabilities and improve the maturity profile of public sector external debt.

By the end of January 1996, Mexico repaid $2 billion of its short-term liabilities to the US Treasury. In August 1996, Mexico prepaid another $7 billion of the loans, and on January 1997, prepaid the remaining $3.5 billion outstanding balance of the loans it had received from the US Treasury. Also, between August 1996 to April 1997, Mexico managed to make early payments of $3.7 billion to the IMF. In total between August 1996 to April 1997, Mexico made early payments of more than one-third of the SDR credit it had received from the IMF.

The ability to return to the international capital markets also enabled Mexico to obtain $949 million through placement of Non-Bank instruments[18] denominated in domestic currency. Part of the funds obtained were used for net amortisation of $103 million Ajustobonos[19] and $156 million Tesobonos[20] which were short-term securities denominated in dollars. Thus, by February 1996, the last Tesobonos in circulation were amortised.

In doing so, as reported by the Bank of Mexico, the Mexican government managed: (1) to reduce the refinancing risk of the public debt denominated in foreign currency; (2) to overcome short-term over indebtedness problem (the Tesobonos problem); (3) to increase the maturity profile of Mexico's public debt from an average of 3.33 years to 7.68 years; and (4) to generate an annual savings of more than $100 million as a result of reduction in the cost of refinanced resources.

In 1996, the external debt of non-bank private sector and commercial banks increased by $1.7 billion. The above figure corresponded to $3.2 billion in net financing obtained by the non-bank private sector, and $1.5 billion amortisation of the external liabilities of commercial banks. In 1996, the flow of direct credits to the non-bank private sector stood at $1.6 billion, of which the net flow from bond placements was $1.3 billion.

Thus it can be seen that the combination of both internal and external rescue packages have been somewhat successful in reviving the Mexican economy. This is particularly apparent when considering the renewed ability of the Mexican public and private sectors in acquiring new funding from the international markets. Overall, compared with the $13.9 billion net outflow in 1995, in 1996 Mexico experienced a net inflow of $908 million, which corresponded to the above $949 million placement of securities by the public sector, and $41 million net payments of commercial banks' loans.

However, it is also important to bear in mind that the remaining internal bad debt and the external debt of banks will continue to exert pressure on both the banking system and the Mexican government for some years to come. By the end of 1996, the gross external debt of commercial banks outstanding amounted to $19.4 billion dollars. Moreover, the new amendments to the regulations will undoubtedly result in further concentration among banks, and within the financial system.

CONCLUDING REMARKS

One of the important shortcomings of the support packages is that the government is not receiving any share of the capital of the banks in return for the supports they provided to the banks. It might have been more appropriate if the government had retained at least some ownership rights in return for the financial assistance they provided. In that way, once the banks were out of difficulty and in profit, the government would at least have some assets in future which could be used to cover the fiscal costs of the packages. The assets that the FOBAPROA has acquired so far are mostly in the form of non-performing loans with very little market value, which may not rise in value in future. The majority of the debtors may continue to have great difficulty in repaying their loans, and in a number of cases, they should in fact be written off all together.

In a market economy, if a company is in difficulty and needs to acquire finance, it would either have to make new share issues, or accept to be taken over by another company who will take over the assets of the failing company, or merge with a stronger company, who will become part owner of the weaker company. In either case, the financiers will acquire some assets, which can be sold in the market at some positive value at some future time. In the case of Mexico, the government provided substantial assistance to the banking sector without acquiring any ownership rights in their capital. It is true that if the government had acquired some ownership rights in return for its financial assistance, then that might have appeared as a somewhat reversal of the earlier privatisation programme. But, acquirement of such part ownership would have at least reduced the costs of debt burden on the public sector, and on future generations, because the government could have sold their shares at a later stage once the banks were out of difficulty. It is important to emphasise that the above practice would not be the same as total reversal of privatisation. This is because while government could have retained some ownership right in return for its assistance it did not have to participate actively in the day-to-day running, and management of the banks. The main objective of such partnership would be the acquisition of some assets for future receipts of income and possibly capital gains once the shares are sold. It is also true that the above form of partnership could give the government a better opportunity to monitor the practices of banks. After all, one of the objectives of privatisation was to increase the public's confidence in the financial system, and ensure depositors of the safety of their deposits.

It is important to note that while in 1992 the government, received 60 billion pesos as a result of sale of the banks, within three years they were obliged to commit themselves to over 210 billion pesos to rescue the same privatised banks form the risk of bankruptcy. A rough calculation clearly indicates that the government not only did not gain as a result of privatisation but also in fact incurred a net loss of 150 billion pesos. Some may argue that the banking crisis of 1995 was due to peso over-valuation, and not poor banking practice. Hence it would have happened irrespective of bank privatisation. Moreover, at least as a result of the privatisation, the government received some one-off income, which helped them to reduce their public sector deficit. Furthermore, because of privatisation, at least part of the burden of banking crisis was born by the private owners of banks.

But on the other hand as a counter argument, it is important to note that had the government not privatised the banks, the level of credits granted by the banks might not have risen as much as they did after privatisation, and the problems of non-performing loans would not have been as bad as they turned out to be. Moreover, the extent by which the public sector's debt dropped after the privatisation was far less than the new fiscal costs of domestic debt relief that is incurred by the government. More importantly, the government would have remained the owner of the banks, and once their difficulty was over, their assets would have once again had a positive value in the market. In addition, the problem of moral hazard in banking practice would not have arisen, as they might have occurred under the present circumstances. It should be pointed out that here the argument is not to re-nationalise the banks, but to acquire some ownership right in return for the costs of rescue packages.

In a private banking system, where the central banks act as a lender of last resort, if a bank finds itself in difficulty, either it would have to bear the costs of poor banking practice through high costs of borrowing from the lender of last resort, or it would be taken over by the lender of last resort who in turn may either sell the bank at a low nominal price in the market, without incurring any of the costs of non-performing loans, or take over the assets and management of the bank and liquidate the banks to pay the creditors and depositors. In either of the above cases, the burden of losses would be born by the shareholders of the bank and possibly the depositors who may not receive their full deposits, rather than the public sector.

In the case of Mexico, however, even though the shareholders have been forced to bear some part of the costs of bank failure, the public sector has committed itself to a larger share of the costs, without retaining any share of the newly injected capital in the bank. In all those packages, assistance was given more in the form of a loan, rather than share-ownership. This has been true in both cases – when the banks were able to survive and when the banks were sold in the market, and the government accepted to take over the entire non-performing loan. In all those cases, while the government provided assistance to both the debtors and the banks, it did not receive any share in banks' new capital in return for its assistance. Whereas as far as the shareholders are concerned, they can at least recover some of their present losses in future once the banking system recovers.

That is why, it may be argued that the manner in which financial assistance has been provided in Mexico has contributed to the spread of moral hazard, among both the private sector debtors and the bankers, who saw that at a time of difficulty the government came to their rescue with hardly any punitive consequences.

In this process, the existing shareholders although they might have incurred some losses at the moment, at least can recover some of their losses in future as they continue being the owners of the banks. The new buyers of the banks are in effect the actual winners of the whole episode, because they have managed to acquire some banks at a rather cheap price, with the government accepting to take over the cost of past-due debt. The public is the ultimate loser and the bearer of the costs of bank failures, in that even though some part of the public have received some form of assistance in repaying their loans, they would ultimately have to repay their debt in the form of future public sector debt burden which would be passed on to them in one way or another, through either higher taxation or lower public expenditure over the next 30 years.

Finally, the present study shows that, although NAFTA played a very important role in rescuing Mexico at the time of its difficulty, it did not play a significant role at the beginning to open the Mexican banking sector to greater foreign competition. The increase in foreign presence in the Mexican banking system that is evident now is in fact merely due to the consequences of the peso crisis, rather than NAFTA. In that respect it is not unreasonable to say that NAFTA contributed to the formation of a more oligopolistic market structure rather than perfect competition. But it is also important to point out that the present crisis, if anything had at least one positive role in that it has pushed Mexico to harmonise its financial regulatory environment and accounting standards more in line with those of other NAFTA members.

Notes

1. The banking sector had been previously nationalised in 1982.
2. The above figures were reported in the Bank of Mexico in 1992.
3. As reported in *The Mexican Economy* (1997), the above figures for 1991 and 1992 exclude non-recurrent revenues derived from privatisation.
4. During the last three years a number of bankers were charged for granting multi-million pesos credits to their own companies. One recent example is Rodriguez Saez who has been arrested in May 1998. In 1991, Rodriguez Saez used front men to buy Banipas (the 8th largest bank in Mexico). Later he used his position at Banipas to authorise credit to companies in which he was the major shareholder with full awareness that the company was in no position to repay the loan. In total he created about $2 billion bad loans for the bank. As a result Banipas was among the first banks to collapse in the 1995 banking crisis.
5. Fundo Bancario de Protección al Ahorro.
6. In this respect, although peso depreciation had an impact on banks' positions its effect was not significant, because the regulation restricted foreign currency exposure of banks to 20 per cent of total liabilities of a bank, and net foreign currency positions was restricted to 15 per cent of net capital.
7. As reported by the *OECD Economic Surveys* (1997), the foreign currency denominated liabilities of the banks' Mexican borrowers increased from 22 per cent at the end of 1993 to 30 per cent at the end of 1994 because of the depreciation of peso. This also reduced the banks' capitalisation ratios because the value of outstanding loans denominated in foreign currency increased.
8. This figure corresponds to the average annual rate of broad unemployment, which was reported by the *Bank of Mexico* in 1997.
9. The North-American Framework Agreement (NAFA) was established in April 1994 to complement series of long-standing bilateral short-term swap arrangements between the US, Canada and Mexico. It provides for enhanced coordination of activities related to bilateral swap arrangements.
10. Unidades de Inversión.
11. Acuerdo de Apoyo Inmediato a los Deudores de la Banco.
12. Acuerdo para el Financiamiento del Sector Agropecuario y Pesquero.
13. Programa de Apoyo a la Micro, Pequeña y Mediana Empresa.
14. Acuerdo para el Financiamiento del Sector Agropecuario y Pesquero.
15. Programa de Apoyo a la Micro, Pequeña y Mediana Empresa.
16. Programme de Capitalización Temporal.
17. Valuación y Venta de Activos, S.A. de C.V.
18. The above securities included $949 million Cetes (which are 28–91 days Treasury bills), $257 million Bondes (which are instruments with interest rates linked to the yield on 28 Day CETES), and 2 million Udibonos (which are long term non-bank instruments indexed to the Consumer Price Index)
19. Long-term non-bank instruments indexed to the Consumer Price Index.
20. Short-term non-bank instruments indexed to the free market exchange rate.

References

Bank of Mexico (1992) *The Mexican Economy 1991*.
Bank of Mexico (1995) *The Mexican Economy 1995*.
Bank of Mexico (1997) *The Mexican Economy 1997*.
Elizondo, Carlos (1993) 'The making of a new alliance: the privatization of the banks in Mexico', Working paper No. 5 (CIDE, Centro De Investigacion Y Docencia Economicas).
Gonzales-Hermosillo, Brenda, Ceyla Pazarbasioglu and Robert Billings (1997) 'Determinants of banking system fragility: a case study of Mexico', *IMF Staff Papers*, vol. 44, no. 3, Sept.
INEGI (1994) *Mexican Bulletin of Statistical Information*, No. 13, July–Sept. (INEGI, Instituto Nacional de Estadistica Geografia e Informatica).
INEGI (1997) *Mexican Bulletin of Statistical Information*, No. 26, Oct.–Dec. (INEGI, Instituto Nacional de Estadistica Geografia e Informatica).
OECD Economic Surveys (1997) (Mexico: OECD).
Perrotini, Ignacio (1996) in Haar, Jerry (ed.) *Financial Services in North America: NAFTA and Beyond* (New Brunswick, NJ: Transaction Books).

3 Private deficit, savings deficit and instability of the Mexican economy[1]

Etelberto Ortiz C.

I THE PROBLEM

For over a decade Mexico has tried to transform its economy, to develop a new economic model, and a new productive organisation that would make it more competitive in the international economy. However, the 1994–95 crisis raised a number of questions about the process of transformation. Though there may be different approaches to the causes of crises, they generally focus around two alternative hypotheses:

- The financial crisis that developed was due to a misconception of the financial model, particularly with respect to the exchange rate and external financing policies.
- The current crisis reveals not only a short-run financial difficulty but also a fundamental shortcoming of the model and policies adopted for structural change.

Under the first hypothesis, it is possible to criticise the financial strategy of 1992 to 1994, particularly with respect to the use of exchange rate as an 'anchor' for the level of prices, where no question is raised on the basic growth model. The second hypothesis though includes a criticism of the exchange rates policies that were adopted, and states that the basic problem was encountered as a result of the pattern of structural change, and the new relationship with the world economy – particularly with the US economy through NAFTA. Therefore, under the second hypothesis, criticism may not necessarily be directed to the need to induce a fundamental change in the productive structure, but to the particular model adopted to induce structural change and the pattern of adjustment so far followed.

This chapter seeks to sustain the second hypothesis in the following way. The first step is to show that the pattern of growth inherently led to the generation of a huge external deficit, and therefore rested on transfers of resources between sectors. The aim was to enhance growth in a few selected sectors, based on their privileged condition with regard to trading conditions and the rate of exchange. This policy produced a 'new dual economy', that will be analysed below in section II. This section concludes that the pattern of growth has been unable to produce a real 'export-led growth' outcome. That is because the leading export sectors are incapable of exerting a positive effect on the rest of the economy. Sections III–V examine the resource transfers that the leading growth sectors are receiving from the rest of the economy. This analysis raises some questions about the very nature of the actual model that is based on the working of a competitive market, but not exempt of the need of subsidies. This pattern has created a new external restriction on the public external debt. That is because although its growth was entirely attributable to a private deficit, it has also been partly financed by public debt. The financial side of the 'new growth model', falls into trouble because it is squeezing domestic savings. In doing so it is generating a permanent state of instability in the Mexican economy. Section VI re-examines critically the theoretical model that has presumably inspired the Mexican model, and section VII offers some tentative conclusions.

II THE NEW 'DUAL ECONOMY'

The pattern of structural change that has been pursued during the last 14 years has created a significant transformation in the Mexican economy. The model has created a new productive structure that is based on exports of the manufacturing sector. The success of the model of structural change is coherent with different rates of growth among various sectors with domestic and export orientation.[2] Table 3.1 shows the rates of growth of GDP and the net export performance of a select group of sectors. The table compares different significant periods in order to highlight the recent outcomes. We observe that though the leading growth sectors experienced a higher rate of growth than the rest of the economy they did not enjoy a corresponding increase in net exports. In fact, we observe that those sectors are primarily responsible for the growth of external deficit after 1988.

Table 3.1 Average rates of growth and rates of net exports to GDP, 1970–93 (sectoral indexes)

	*Average rate of growth**					*Average share of net exports to GDP***				
Sector	*70–76*	*77–81*	*82–87*	*88–93*	*88–95*	*70–76*	*77–81*	*82–87*	*88–93*	*88–95*
Total	5.9	10.5	–0.1	3.2	2.5	–4.4	–2.2	6.6	–0.7	–4.7
Leading sectors	7.7	11.1	6.6	5.7	5.5	–24.3	–25.2	**–2.3**	**10.0**	**–16.5**
Primary	2.6	5.1	1.4	1.0	1.7	1.3	–4.1	–3.4	–4.6	–0.0
Extractive	6.7	–0.1	0.4	1.1	1.0	7.9	94.8	211.5	182.1	–1.5
Food industry	4.6	7.5	0.9	4.0	3.7	15.3	–1.1	7.3	–1.8	–6.5
Light industry	5.0	7.7	–1.3	0.1	1.9	–18.3	–19.2	–16.0	–17.1	–40.4
Chemical and petrochemical	9.4	4.4	2.5	3.4	2.4	–51.7	–26.0	–4.6	–14.7	–27.5
Iron ore industries	6.7	11.6	1.6	3.3	2.4	–8.6	–28.8	–1.5	–3.0	3.9
Motor cars and others	8.3	13.4	–1.0	6.9	2.6	**–66.9**	**–61.3**	**–23.4**	**–51.4**	**–39.0**
Services	5.8	8.1	0.8	2.4	2.3	–0.0	–0.1	–0.6	0.0	–0.0
Hotels, restaurants and transport	8.8	10.9	–1.0	5.9	2.7	0.0	0.0	–0.0	0.0	0.0
Construction	6.5	14.2	–4.2	4.4	0.9	0.0	0.0	0.0	0.0	0.0
Retail	5.9	17.3	–1.8	2.3	0.3	0.0	0.0	0.0	0.0	0.0

Notes: * Average rate of growth, per year, GDP.
** Average share of the trade balance, (exports–imports), to GDP for each sector (72 sectors, NIPA).
Source: *National Income and Product Accounts (NIPA) 1970–1995*, Published by Instituto Nacional de Estadistica Geografia e Informatica (INEGI).

A unique characteristic of the new structure of production is that successful exporters make profits on the basis of imported inputs. This condition is extreme in the case of the motor cars, electronics and capital equipment industries. Non-tradable sectors also performed reasonably well in terms of their contribution towards GDP growth. It is also remarkable that net exports remain within the domain of primary and extractive sectors. These phenomena can also be detected through the change in the total linkage coefficients. Table 3.2 provides an estimate of the linkage coefficients of the leading sectors with the whole economy.

The drop in the linkage coefficients of the motor car and motor parts industry, and others, such as electronics, is remarkable. However, they were not an exception, as similar changes can also be observed in sectors such as petrochemicals, cement and glass, that provide the bulk of the export income.

Productivity and employment follows the same path. Leading growth sectors are also at the forefront of productivity and performance league. This success, however, can be essentially explained by drops in the rate of employment and changes in relative prices.[3]

Table 3.2 Total linkage coefficients Mexican economy (1950–95)

Sector	*1950*	*1960*	*1970*	*1980*	*1985*	*1988*	*1990*	*1995p*
Agriculture	1.48	1.56	1.85	1.82	1.77	2.29	1.99	1.99
Oil and gas	1.29	1.92	2.62	1.68	1.67	2.79	1.58	1.58
Food industry	1.2	1.33	1.29	1.27	1.13	1.76	1.16	1.16
Beer			1.13	1.10	1.05	1.06	1.06	1.05
Glass			1.91	1.85	1.77	1.77	1.62	1.49
Cement			2.12	1.98	1.92	2.08	1.82	1.81
Petrochemical			3.28	2.936	4.45	4.06	2.66	2.61
Motor cars		1.18	1.12	1.12	1.08	1.064	1.038	1.02
Motor parts			2.23	**2.17**	**1.60**	**1.367**	**1.44**	**1.28**
Electricity	1.10	2.02	2.24	2.385	2.49	2.86	2.49	2.63
Transport and communications	1.17	1.51	1.52	1.44	1.49	1.20	1.40	1.40
Hotels and restaurants	1.00	1.15	1.21	1.22	1.21	1.17	1.22	1.25
Services	1.22	1.35	1.37	1.32	1.33	1.51	1.44	1.46
Retail	1.17	1.34	1.47	1.31	1.34	1.45	1.32	1.35
Average	2.31	1.69	1.80	1.745	1.71	1.84	1.62	1.61
Std Dev.	1.74	0.47	0.65	0.613	0.67	0.79	0.56	0.57

Note: *Stata Matrix*, Consultoria Internacional Especializada, S.A. de C.V. Mexico 1990, 1995.
Source: Ortiz (1994), p. 139. Preliminary estimates for 1990–95.

The paradox of the success of the model is that it identifies the 'winners' on the basis of their position in the world economy, even though the objective was to create a new pattern that was not based on the hypothesis of 'convergence', either domestically or with the world economy. Therefore, the growth of the export sector is not necessarily associated with the growth of the economy and the net income of exports. Thus, we conclude that *the success of structural change policies has been to create a new dual economy*, where one sector is based on cheap imported inputs that are predominantly used in production of goods destined for the international market, and another sector that is based on cheap labour and is oriented towards the domestic market. The macroeconomic implications of this fact are still to be discussed.

III PRIVATE DEFICIT AND STRUCTURAL CHANGE

External debts have been generally attributed to public deficits. That was true of the deficits during the 1970s and the early 1980s. But that is not the case today. The 1994–95 foreign exchange crisis in Mexico was entirely attributable to a private sector trade deficit, generated by the leading growing manufacturing sector. This problem should be approached from the relationship between economic growth and net exports and its finances. That is because, while domestic prices were kept under control, and import prices grew faster than export prices,[4] the real value of exports grew by 8 per cent, which was half as fast as the real value of imports which grew by 17 per cent.

The external deficit was generated by some of the growing manufacturing sectors, which were the leaders in the structural transformation from 1989 to 1994. These were responsible for over 78 per cent of the trade deficit,[5] and were among the few sectors that showed increases in productivity and output. However, compared to 1985–87, it can also be observed that, although the above sectors increased their manufacturing exports at an unprecedented level, the rate of growth of exports as a whole, and the share of manufacturing exports of GDP, has been decreasing between 1987 and 1990. That has been the case except for a few occasions when sudden increases have been observed. The difficulty is that from 1990 onwards, the increase in the rate of manufacturing exports has been achieved through a massive increase in imports of intermediate inputs.

The notion of a 'private deficit' is concerned with the problem of dealing with an appraisal of real growth in the economy, and the position of privileged sectors. The difficulty here is that the data on the actual value of commodities produced with imported items is misleading. In order to assess properly the real price of those commodities, it has to be assumed that the rate of exchange is an equilibrium rate. In other words, the exchange rate should be expressed as the actual opportunity cost of imported items. In that case the value of imported inputs would correspond to its opportunity cost. That is, it would be equal to the value of the commodities exported, in the amount necessary to pay for those imports. This view is relevant, because we are dealing with the assessment of the long run properties of a peculiar growth model, one that rests on a critical relationship with the world economy.

Therefore, the notion of a 'private deficit' is related to the difference between the social cost and the private cost of imported items that are used as inputs in the production of exports. The 'private deficit' is equivalent to the difference between the nominal value of imported inputs and its real value at e^*, which presumably should approach its opportunity cost.

Therefore, the fact that the exchange rate in Mexico tends to be overvalued shows that the problem is not just a matter of short run adjustment. The 1990–94 experience was particularly dramatic in that respect.

The difficulty about the real value of imported inputs is that, if they are undervalued, firms are not charging the real opportunity cost of the resources involved in their production. It might not be evident that firms do not pay the difference. Their import costs are lower because the actual exchange rate reduces their costs. Therefore, there is no reason to reduce their imports. Evidently, the difference in exchange rates amounts to imports subsidy, and poses a long run problem in terms of allocation of resources and valuation of production. However, the end result may not be all that evident. Therefore, in spite of the profits made in those sectors, we have two basic difficulties with respect to the real cost of resources:

- There is a distortion that gives a privilege to sectors whose advantages in trade and growth are dubious. This is at the cost of sectors with a higher potential in terms of growth, exports and employment. The difference rests on preserving a new duality in the economy. Some sectors will survive on the basis of low wages and not on an international competitive drive.

- There is a deficit that is caused by private decisions of production, but does not appear in private balances. These in fact show a profit. But the real deficit that appears as the trade deficit is turned into public debt.

In order to show the magnitude of that deficit, even as a rough estimate, we assessed the difference of imports at a constant real exchange rate of 1986, when the external account was almost in equilibrium[6] Table 3.3 presents the impacts from 1970 to 1994. We find that sectors 23 to 32, 33 to 42 and 48 to 59, produced almost 80 per cent of the whole deficit. It is remarkable that those sectors are the same as those that led the export growth and expanded faster.

The last three columns present a real paradox. They show that the cost of transfers under the 'export-led growth model' in fact increased compared to the previous period. The second row, shows that the leading growing sectors, under the new model, which is supposedly market-oriented without 'price distortions', increased the transfers considerably instead of reducing it. The increased cost is even more than the cost observed during the period of import substitution industrialisation.

Table 3.3 Assessment of the private deficit, attributable to the 1986 equilibrium rate of exchange (1970–95)

	Private deficit (% GDP)					
Sector	*70–76*	*77–81*	*82–87*	*88–93*	*88–94*	*88–95*
Total	−4.8	−6.1	−1.5	−6.6	−7.4	−6.3
Leading sectors	−16.5	−22.2	−5.0	**−30.0**	**−38.2**	**−32.6**
Primary	−3.4	−6.2	−2.0	−4.5	−5.6	−4.8
Extractive	−5.1	3.6	−0.7	−3.2	−3.5	−3.0
Food industry	−2.3	−5.3	−1.4	−8.3	−10.7	−9.1
Light industry	−16.8	−17.6	−4.5	−25.3	−36.2	−30.7
Chemical and petrochemical	−22.4	−24.0	−7.3	**−25.8**	**−32.5**	**−27.7**
Iron ore industries	−10.8	−23.9	−4.1	−14.4	−17.6	−15.0
Motor cars and others	−43.3	−51.5	−12.7	**−54.8**	**−57.5**	**−49.1**
Services	−0.0	−0.0	−0.0	−0.0	−0.0	−0.0
Non-tradables	0	0	0	0	0	0

Source: *National Income and Product Accounts, 1970–1995*, and author elaboration.

From an orthodox neoclassical approach, it might be argued that the policy of fixing of the exchange rate was the right choice, particularly in view of the pressures to stabilise prices and the push for structural change through trade liberalisation. The difficulty with that policy was not just that it ignored the extent of the impact of trade liberalisation on the economy in terms of the needs for foreign exchange. The basic problem was that the policy mix, trade liberalisation and overvaluation of the exchange rate distorted the whole environment in which the policies of structural change operated. A far-reaching consequence was that there was no way by which the private enterprises could identify the real value of their inputs, and therefore their products.

This analysis of the exchange rate reveals a hidden idea in the minds of the policy-makers, a rather traditional one. That is, trade liberalisation would create a huge demand for imports at any rate of exchange; therefore the balance of payments deficit would persist for sometime anyway. Furthermore, the requirement of imports could not be regulated through the standard supply and demand mechanism.

Another factor also encouraged the adoption of that policy. The way in which the process of structural change was taking place set a condition in which domestic economy could in no way provide the particular inputs that were required by the growth sector at competitive prices. That was particularly due to the introduction of new technologies and production processes inter-linked on a world scale that was introduced by intra-firm trade – a condition relevant for an important share of trade within the manufacturing sector, particularly for the leading growing sectors.

True, this behaviour may be attributed to an overvalued rate of exchange. Enterprises just profited out of the opportunity at hand. But it seems that the view of public officials, from the very beginning, was that price stabilisation was a top priority. Therefore, with financial liberalisation ignored, the attack on inflation created a cumulative effect on external debt. The 1994–95 crisis was the evidence that the model was untenable in terms of its finances. Our contention is that it also showed that the very model of structural change was not working properly.

The coincidence of both events, growth and external deficit in the same sectors, is not an accident. They reflect a structural behavior that has been pointed out in many forms, i.e. the impossibility of growth of the Mexican economy without generating a trade deficit, the marginal propensity to import well over unity, the very small degree of integration of our industry, structural and technological dependence, etc.

But the problem rests on the way the process of structural change has been conceived and constructed. In transferring from a closed to an open economy, it is expected that some sectors should produce an excess of exports over imports, while the lagging sectors might create an excess of imports over exports. Either a comparative advantage or a dynamic competitive advantage may explain the position of the 'winners'.[7] But, in any case whether it is due to resource availability or technological drive, the model should work if and only if, those sectors that take the lead in productivity and growth are the same sectors that provide the flow of exports. Furthermore, the process is expected to work from the impulse of exports to its impact on growth over all. The other important effect is even more relevant. It is expected that the sectors devoid of competitive capabilities turn into 'losers', and that they should end up disappearing, or at least turn into net importers. The model would be successful if the growth induced by the first group exceed the losses of the second.

For the Mexican economy, evidence shows that the process has worked in reverse, particularly with respect to the relationship between exporters and the net importing sectors. It has been shown that the leading growth sectors not only are producing the current account deficit but also their exports are not associated with the overall growth in the manufacturing sector. Furthermore, the observed increase in productivity is associated with the changes in relative prices, and not with the size of exports.[8]

Consequently, under these conditions, trade deficits have a particular meaning. They correspond to an income deficit, in so far as those enterprises that import more than they export are not paying for the full cost of their inputs. The cost of that deficit is entirely transferred to society due to the public action of absorbing the debt caused by the trade deficit.[9]

IV PRIVATE DEFICIT, EXTERNAL DEBT, AND DOMESTIC SAVINGS

Perhaps the magnitude of the present financial crisis cannot be explained purely by the productive behaviour. Nor can it be explained by the overvalued exchange rate. The situation is in fact also related to the process of financial liberalisation, which was a factor that did not help to stabilise the difficulties of management of the productive deficit. Indeed, the financial contour was a factor that magnified instability. Our inquiry is directed to the fact that the urge to obtain short run finance to back the trade deficit and honour the external debt, worked severely against the model of structural change in another form. It destroyed domestic savings, damped the rate of investment, and consequently reduced the long run capabilities of growth.

This problem has generally been reduced to the magnitude of external debt and its financial service. Our perception, however, is that it also involved other difficulties. It is evident that, in spite of the successive debt re-negotiations, the overall process did not lead to a reduction of the external service but made it bigger, as can be appreciated in Table 3.4. There, in column 4, the real impact of debt service is made evident when it is evaluated in terms of a real exchange rate.

Table 3.4 External debt service share of GDP in nominal terms and corrected by the 1986 real exchange rate

Year	*Service ($m)*	*Share of GDP nominal*	*Share of GDP (1986 Real rate)*
1980	9,081.0	4.66	7.34
1981	13,189.4*	5.28	9.84
1982	17,631.7	10.29	14.03
1983	14,592.3	12.27	15.59
1984	14,068.5	8.84	13.55
1985	13,017.2	8.52	13.52
1986	11,142.5	8.94	9.71
1987	11,349.3	8.28	8.28
1988	11,942.1	6.57	7.99
1989	12,915.6	5.84	7.72
1990	12,398.6	4.76	6.30
1991	15,925.3	5.06	7.44
1992	20,833.3	5.73	9.18
1993	22,386.9	5.73	9.34
1994	27,031.4	6.20	9.02
1995	44,900.7	15.71	15.82
1996	39,921.0	11.93	13.03
1997	39,061.0	10.34	12.98

Source: The Ministry of the Treasury (SHCP) (1997) and Bank of Mexico (1997).

The difficulty we are concerned with is the relationship between the private deficit and its financing on the basis of an ever increasing debt and its service. This phenomenon pervades the whole process of growth, because the external finance of the private deficit ended up reducing the domestic private saving.

The Mexican experience also shows that in spite of the large magnitude of capital resources that went into the country, sooner or later those capitals had to be backed by public debt. That is evident with the sudden change in the level of external debt, which was generated by private enterprises and private banks. Once they were facing the risk of default, their liabilities had to be very quickly converted into public debt.

In Table 3.4, the nature of the new debt is expressed not only in terms of its share of GDP in nominal terms but also when it is adjustment in terms of the 1986 real exchange rate. The basic impact of the new debt can be appraised in its servicing (capital payments and interests). In 1995, the external service, when added by the conversion of 'Tesobonos', were well over 15 per cent of the new level of GDP (considering devaluation, and a 5 per cent contraction in GDP in real terms). Considering the schedule of payments, it is evident that will not fall below 11 per cent for at least five years. Once it returns to its long run trend, until the year 2000, it would be unlikely to fall below 11 per cent of GDP if the present trends continue to prevail.

The difficulty with this form of financing of the external deficit can be appraised when we observe its two other impacts. The first impact was in terms of transforming short-term private debts into long-term public debt. The second one is the destruction of private savings, which is very important in the analysis of the instability of the Mexican economy.

This can be observed if we consider the difference between the total savings, direct saving plus depreciation, less external savings, including foreign investment and capital flows, and public savings.[10] This will give the residual amount of private domestic savings. Table 3.5 shows the estimation for all these variables.

The dramatic drop in domestic savings corresponds to a twofold behaviour:

- With the small rate of investment and the massive flow of short-term external capital, the economy in fact behaved as if it were in the presence of an excess of savings over investment.

Table 3.5 Gross national savings, external, public and external, gross rate of investment (as a % of GDP) (1980–97)

Year	*Gross fixed investment*	*Gross national saving*[1]	*External saving*[2]	*Net external saving*[3]	*Public saving*[4]	*Private saving*[5]
1980	24.8	23.6	1.74	4.46	−1.1	24.16
1981	26.4	24.5	1.97	9.74	−7.5	32.00
1982	22.2	27.9	−5.79	−4.64	−0.3	28.20
1983	16.6	27.2	−1.66	−17.51	7.5	19.70
1984	17.0	26.2	−9.13	−9.28	3.3	22.90
1985	17.9	24.2	−6.27	−10.35	−0.2	24.40
1986	16.4	22.2	−5.74	−8.46	−5.3	27.50
1987	16.1	23.6	−7.51	−7.02	−4.0	27.60
1988	19.0	21.8	−2.77	−7.38	−3.8	25.60
1989	21.0	22.1	−1.10	−5.00	−3.7	**25.80**
1990	22.1	22.0	0.08	1.91	−1.1	**23.10**
1991	22.7	20.7	1.98	4.10	0.8	**19.90**
1992	23.1	18.6	4.44	2.81	2.0	**16.60**
1993	21.0	17.6	3.41	5.60	1.0	**16.50**
1994	21.6	16.9	4.70	−3.43	−0.1	**17.00**
1995	17.7	21.9	−4.24	−6.04	0.7	**21.9**
1996	16.1	19.2	−3.16	−6.35	0.3	19.2
1997P	18.0	16.9	−1.91	−1.0	−2.1	19.00

Note: p = preliminary estimate
Source: [1] *National Income and Product Accounts (NIPA) 1980–1997*; [2] Trade deficit + net non-factorial income + interest received by domestic residents; [3] Net endebtment + foreign investment + foreign debt service. Balance of Payments, 1980–1997, Bank of Mexico; [4] Estimated as Public balance + Inflation tax, the Minstry of the Treasury (SHCP) and Bank of Mexico (1997); [5] Is obtained as a residual.

- Given the current account deficit, the economy had to reduce its rate of growth in order to accommodate the flows of external savings.

Both phenomena are evident in the increase of the average and marginal propensity to consume, which was observed between 1989 and 1994. But it is also evident in the way the financial sector managed to profit from the foreign exchange rate at a low price, and financial resources that were made available at low rates accommodated to pay very high rates of interest in the domestic market.

All these resulted in a reduction of the rate of domestic savings and the collapse of the rate of investment. It should be stressed that both of these impacts were the consequence of financial liberalisation.

The increase in external savings, though increased financial deepening, could not do much to increase financial savings throughout the period.

The way in which the Central Bank managed the sterilisation of external savings created a massive impulse for over borrowing within the domestic financial market. The consequence was the increase of the domestic rate of interest and of bad loans in early 1993.

V STAGNATION, FINANCIAL INSTABILITY AND CRISIS

A growth model essentially should have an answer to two basic issues:

- Priorities for growth, which generally means determining the sectors that will take a leading roll for growth.
- The way in which it is to be financed.

Experience and theory shows that the above questions are not independent. Our query is not on the presumable advantages of 'export-led growth' models. The problem is with the actual model according to which the Mexican economy is being run. The finance of a 'private deficit economy' is that it demands somebody to take the external deficit in order for those sectors to make a profit and grow. *Such a model is untenable by all standards*. Those leading sectors account for only 8.5 per cent of GDP, and affect an even smaller proportion of workers. Therefore it can be asserted that the above strategy is too expensive and not efficient enough to promote the improvement and welfare of the population.

There is a last consideration about the nature of the model and its finances. The provision of external resources to finance the balance of payments deficit demanded a profound distortion in the capital market. The price to pay to attract $24 billion for three consecutive years was not just to face a very high rate of interest in contracting additional resources, but it also meant that the economy was thrown in to a slump process, as the rate of GDP growth collapsed from 5 per cent in 1990 to 1 per cent in 1993.

An important factor that contributed to that situation was the role of financial intermediaries in magnifying the impacts of external flows. Looking for external savings, they managed to obtain resources at high rates by international standards, and allocated them to the domestic market at even higher rates. This difference in interest rates cannot be reduced to the term structure of interest rates on the basis of different risk and other conditions. This behaviour soon started to show that, in fact, they were playing different roles, according to their size and international relationship. Export leaders and banks could obtain lower rates than the rest of the economy. Consequently, they were not facing a problem with respect to the rate of exchange, or rates of interest. For the rest of the economy, however, the above factors pushed them into a permanent recessive drive.

Conventional theory supports the idea that the contraction in the rate of growth of the economy may be a logical result of events such as those that have been described in this chapter. But, given the way in which the particular model operated in Mexico, our contention is that, ex-ante, the model worked backwards. In other words, *the decision was to induce a very slow growth in the economy in order to produce the overall change associated with the financial liberalisation of the economy*.

Structural change was displaced as a secondary policy target in order to force down the rate of inflation, and create a 'financial paradise' for international capital. The image of 'modernisation' through NAFTA and financial liberalisation, reinforced each other, in such a way that 'reputation' was considered enough to attract more capitals. But the limit was imposed right from the beginning. Exports lagged behind imports, and the investment coefficient remained around the average rate of the former 10 years.

Therefore, one cannot argue that the model for structural change that was followed during the last 12 years was a viable project in terms of its dynamism or its impact on employment. The result was:

- Financial instability due to the inability of domestic producers to pay for the very high real rates of interest – to the extent that the size of bank defaults was increasing in 1993, long before the crisis appeared.
- Despite the falling rate of economic growth between 1991 to 1993,[11] imports were consistently growing, even faster than exports and consequently the trade deficits were rising.
- The extent of private banks' external indebtedness over-exposed their financial stability, as was evident in January 1995. This situation was also encouraged by the inability of the authorities to sterilise the massive flows of external capital. Consequently, some of those banks have been taken over by foreign concerns and indirectly by public resources.

- Excess profits in the banking sector were not enough to clear banks' need to cover their capital balance. Though the share of financial sector of GDP doubled between 1989 to 1994, from 7 per cent to 15 per cent respectively, the increase in bad loans in just two years, 1993–94, was such that by the end of 1994 banks were in default.
- The reduction of the rate of inflation was always misleading. In fact Mexico had a 'repressed inflation'. That is, agents in the economy had a considerable pressure to adjust prices, but foreign competition frustrated their efforts to differentiate prices. The fact that the adjustment was not over is evident by the fact that in spite of the fall in the rate of inflation, efforts to differentiate prevailed ever since 1989.

All of those events worked against the efforts for structural change. But it also has to be highlighted that they worked against the objective of building a competitive financial sector that could provide the necessary savings for growth. It is evident that there was a need to put together both projects of structural change and financial efficiency. The adjustment pattern that was adopted, however, did not necessarily provide a consistent solution for both. McKinnon's criticism rests on the parsing of both processes. The evidence of the Mexican economy shows that the reason why the model does not work is because it rests on the need of private deficits and income transfers that make it untenable, and not because of the parsing of structural change and financial liberalisation.

VI THEORETICAL ISSUES

During the 1970s and early 1980s, Mexico experienced a huge increase in its external debt, due to policies of excess public expenditures and mismanagement of capital flows and rates of exchange that led to massive capital outflows. Now we have a new process that has led to a huge increase in external debt. But there is one difference; the present indebtedness is entirely attributable to private deficits that are generated as a result of a 'pure market model'.

The government argued that the financial crisis of 1994–95 was because 'private investors had identified that the trade deficit could no longer be sustained by short-term transfers of capital and public debt'.[12] Such an argument amounts to saying that, after 4 months of capital flight, everybody in the world was well aware of the situation, except the Mexican government. But it also shows a total unawareness of the nature of this crisis. The policy response that has followed clearly does not respond to the true nature of a 'private deficit economy'. The 1998 financial crisis showed once again the vulnerability of the economy because it continued to work on the same model.

What kind of theory helps best to understand all those problems? A non-trivial approach requires giving an answer to the following problems:

Here we have a case of a totally open economy, which has to work in the context of a 'successful export-led growth model'. Nevertheless, against its ideal characteristics, the model rests on the creation of deficits and transfers that call for an increase in public indebtedness. Within an orthodox model it is impossible to distinguish between the social and private costs, in view of the free operation of market forces. A consistent theoretical approach needs to give account of the impossibility to behave according to the essential hypothesis of the orthodox model: *the convergence towards international standards and the creation of a homogeneous economy*. Any viable approach would have to give an answer to the success of this market model: *A new dual economy*. This new dual economy presents two mutually interrelated aspects: the 'real side', which out of its trade and productive relationships creates the 'private deficit', and the financial side, with a segmented structure depending on the external insertion of agents, with one rate of exchange but two rates of interest.

To what extent is it possible to say that overvaluation was a misconceived policy? That is, as a case of market failure that is induced by policy errors? Such a case is entirely parallel to saying that overvaluation was the right policy for the purpose of creating the impulse for a peculiar growth model, or an export-led growth model that was based on 'maquila' production. If it were assessed in that form, then there was no error in policy at all. In that case, the policy adopted was aimed consistently. But it would no longer is a case of 'market failure'.

A line of criticism to the basic model that was followed, that is the Mundell–Fleming model, has developed from the analysis of the characteristics of the capital market. The aim is to present a critique of the basic framework, i.e. the IS–LM model for an open economy.

The essential message is that, even within the context of a fully fledged model of 'sound fundamentals', the working of the capital market, instead of conducting the economy towards the full equilibrium,

Figure 3.1

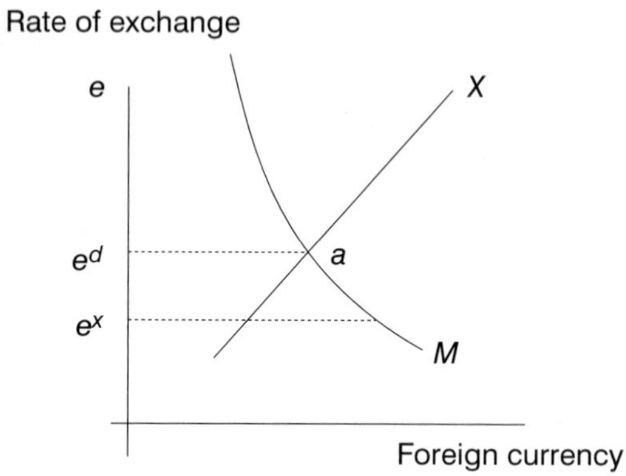

Figure 3.2

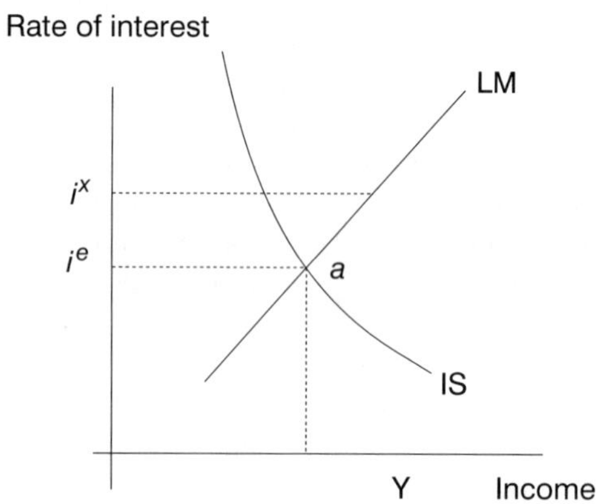

induces the abandonment of 'sound macroeconomic fundamentals', as is presented in Figures 3.1 and 3.2

Here we can observe that profit maximisation in the capital market, conducted by the principle of reducing and equalising risks in all the instruments, might induce capital flows to such an extent that provoke the distortion on interest rates and exchange rates, Cornfold and Kregel (1996). Then, the successful operation of the capital market induces to go away from equilibrium at point a, turning against all the effort and social costs of sustaining 'sound macroeconomic fundamentals'.

An alternative line of criticism here is developed, still on the basis of a Mundell–Fleming model, but considering two characteristics:

1. The particular structural conditions of an economy like the Mexican model, which is characterised by:

- structural duality in the productive sector, particularly the condition that one sector seems to be operating on one set of prices (i.e. exchange rate, international rates of interest and human capital), while another sector is associated with a different price vector (i.e. low wages, and cheap capital expenses);
- heavy external debt service;
- the leading growth sectors that necessarily generate a deficit, in foreign currency and in the savings ratio.

2. The successful operation of the capital market that leads to massive inflows of external savings within a context of a very thin capital market, inadequate for the sterilisation of massive flows of external capital. There is a macroeconomic bifurcation in the capital market, represented by two sectors, the export leaders who obtain low rates of interest in the international market, and domestic producers who have to face high rates of interest.

The essentials of the criticism is that structural condition (1) means that there is a dichotomised pricing behaviour, because agents are confronted with two different sets of prices: one that is relevant for the leading growing–exporting sectors, P_x and another one for the domestic-oriented sector, P_d. The paradox is that the above outcome is the result of a model of liberalisation of trade and investment, and of an economy that is fully open to international trade. Therefore, even if agents can observe one single price vector, that includes both P_x and P_d, productive agents have access to just one of them. The dichotomy arises from the full operation of a global economy. It is not a case of 'market failure' where institutional limitations or price rigidities give way to discriminatory conditions. The price dichotomy arises from the possibility that agents may have different strategies towards profit optimisation in the market. Consequently, different patterns of production may arise. This case is based on the nature of a transnational production model, where actual patterns of integration respond to profit maximising in relation to the international and domestic markets, through intra-firm trade. This particular model might be identified as the 'maquila model'.

Condition (2) leads to market segmentation in the capital market, which given the form of operation of financial intermediaries, is transformed into over-borrowing and increasing financial fragility. A first form of representation of such a model, within a neoclassical framework is as follows:

The production function of the leading export sectors, x is the following:

$$Q_x = f_x(K_x, H_x, M)$$

subject to the budget constraint:

$$B_x = rK_x + whH + EMP^*$$

such that $f_x'(K) > 0, f_x'(H) > 0, f_x''(K) < 0, f_x''(H) < 0$. And the production function for the domestic market, d.

$$Q_d = f_d(K_d, L_d, Q_d)$$

subject to the budget constraint:

$$B_d = rK_d + wL + Q_dP_d$$

such that $f_d'(K) > 0,\ f_d'(L) > 0,\ f_d''(K) < 0,\ f_d''(L) < 0$.

Where, Q represents commodities, either as outputs or inputs, K is capital, H is human capital, M is imported inputs, L is labour, E is the nominal rate of exchange, P is price, r is the price of capital, w is the wage rate, and B is the total budget constraint for each sector. Sub-indices are related to the two sectors. First derivatives are shown with one prime, and second derivatives with two primes.

The demand vectors are:

Leading export sectors

Demand for consumption goods is given by: $D_{dx} = C_{cx}(Y_d, e)$
$= c_{cx}Q_x + M_{xd}$

Demand for investment goods is given by: $I_x = I_x(Y_u, i^*) = M_{xi}$

And the demand for exportable is given by: $X = X(Y_u, E(P^*/P))$,

Aggregate demand for sector x is: $Y_x = P_xQ_x = D_x + I_x + X$
Therefore: $Y_x = P_xQ_x = d_x[Y_d, Y_u, i^*, E(P^*/P)]$
And aggregate supply for this sector is: $O_x = P_xQ_x + M_{xd} + M_{xi}$

Domestic market sector
Demand for consumption goods is given by: $D_d = C_d(W/P)$
Demand for investment goods is given by: $I_d = I_d(Y, i_d)$
The aggregate demand vectors is: $Y_d = P_dQ_d = D_d + I_d$
Therefore: $Y_d = P_dQ_d = d_d[Y_d, i_d, W/P]$
And the aggregate supply vector is given by: $O_d = P_dQ_d + M_{dc} + M_{di}$

Where, Y is the national income; i is the rate of interest, I is total investment, i^* is the international rate of interest, Y_u is the national income in the rest of the world (or in the US), $E(P^*/P)$ is the real exchange rate $= e$, M is total imports and (W/P) is the real wage.

The standard equation of demand for money is established upon the liquidity preference theory: $M_o = M_dh[Y, i]$, with the usual properties: $h'[Y] > 0$; and $h'[i] < 0$.

Given that differentiated demand behaviour might have an incidence, marginal propensities to consume in each sector may be different. Considering the Engel's law, the marginal propensities to consume in each sector are: $0 < c_x'(Y) < 1$ and $0 < c_d'(W/P) < 1$, we could expect: $c_x'(Y) < c_d'(W/P])$. If additionally we assume that $I_x'(i^*) < 0$, and $I_d'(i) < 0$, We can say that there are two IS curves, which at a given particular exchange rate E, have the following slopes:

For the leading export sector, x:

$$\mathrm{IS}_x = \left[\frac{c_x i^* + I_x i^*}{I - c_x}\right]$$

For the domestic market sector, d:

$$\mathrm{IS}_d = \left[\frac{I_d i}{I - c_d}\right]$$

Under the standard assumptions, we should expect the slop of the IS curve of the leading export sectors to be smaller than that of the domestic market. The size of the markets is also reflected, considering that the domestic market for an economy is expected to be bigger than the export market. Consequently, under a particular profile of monetary policy, which is in terms of the demand for money curve, the

Figure 3.3 Macroeconomic dual structure

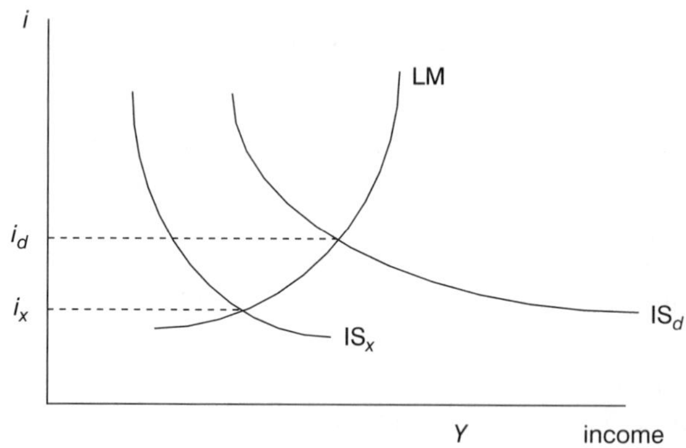

model may be represented by a dichotomised macroeconomic structure as in Figure 3.3.

Evidently for each IS curve a different level of income prevails, which corresponds to each sector of the economy. It is assumed that the domestic sector is bigger than the exporting sector, and it also shows more elasticity in its slop. The essential difference is that for each segment of the economy in fact we find a different rate of interest, though given the size and the elasticity characteristics, we should expect that the rate for the domestic sector should be higher than the one feasible for the leading export sectors. This should not be much different from that of the rest of the world.

It is important to highlight that there are many theoretical aspects to a model like this, which could be analysed, for example, with respect to growth trajectories, productivity, etc. Nevertheless, in spite of their importance, they will not be tackled here. For the time being we shall be concerned with the initial problem of our inquiry, i.e. the inner characteristics of instability of the model.

The interesting aspect of a dichotomised macroeconomic structure, based on differentiation of the 'real sector', in the form of two IS curves, is in the analysis of the dynamic characteristics that such a model imposes on the exchange and monetary policy. The purpose is to show the inadequacies of the current view on the actual operation of the economy.

The standard view is that on the right of the IS we have an excess supply, in the commodities market, i.e. $S > I$, while on the left we should find the reverse, i.e. $S < I$. Accordingly, for the money market, on the right and below the LM curve we have an excess demand for money, i.e. $M_d > M_0$. Let us put aside the discussion of other models on exchange rate dynamics.[13] The dynamics of this model with the two IS curves is not limited to the impact of a particular rate of interest, which would mean an excess demand for one sector, or an express an excess supply of the other.

To give a full appraisal of the model, we obtain the internal and external balance curves from the balance of payments equation. These curves are formed considering the aggregation of the total transactions of the economy. That is, those from the balance of trade, and capital account of the balance of payments. Therefore, for a particular rate of interest, we can derive the locus of exchange rates and income that are compatible with internal balance (IB) and external balance (EB). The first two terms in the balance of payments equation correspond to the trade balance, and the last term corresponds to the capital account:

$$\mathrm{BP} = \xi(Y) + \gamma(e) + \sigma(i - i^*, e)$$

Figure 3.4 External and internal disequilibrium

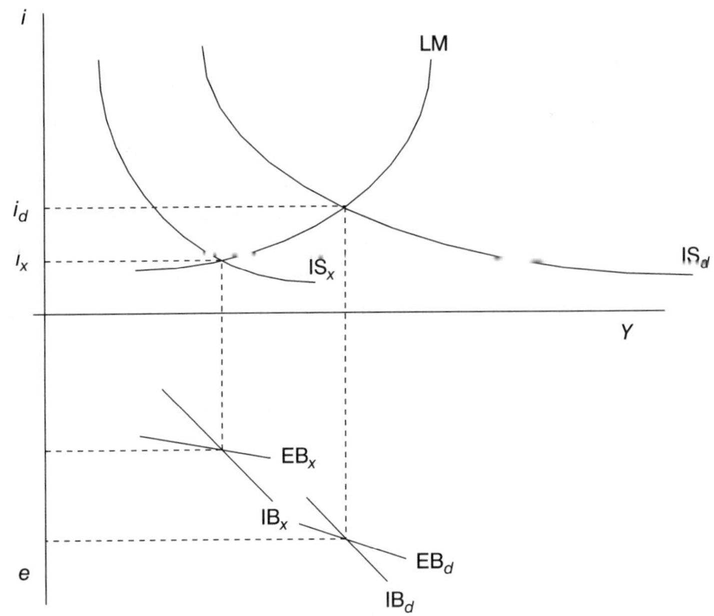

The essential difficulty to be observed is in the dichotomy between the whole set of internal and external equilibrium conditions for each pair $[E, i]$. Considering that an open economy can have only one exchange rate, the model here requires the presence of two rates of interest. The higher rate, while indicating an excess supply of savings for the export sector, represents a very restrictive condition for the domestic sector. Overall, the model while creates conditions of stagnation in the economy, but at the same time generates conditions of excess savings over investment.

Furthermore, it can also be observed that each pair of $(i–e)$ are coherent with one another. But the question then is, whether there exists one condition that could favour the imposition of just one of them. Market forces in a small economy open to trade would be expected to follow conditions of the external sector, particularly on the exchange rate. Macroeconomic bifurcation means that at e^*, even if that were an equilibrium rate for the export sector, the exchange rate would be overvalued from the point of view of the domestic market. The second condition on rates of interest, with $i^* > i_d$, would recreate recessive conditions for the domestic sector.

VII TENTATIVE CONCLUSIONS

If globalisation were to be understood as the prevalence of one single price vector all over the world that does not necessarily mean that every agent in the world can have access to every single commodity. Differences in capabilities and industrial relationships create differences in the conditions of production. The essential differences surge from the technology and capital markets. At a macroeconomic level, it means that two dichotomised sectors will be operating, with two rates of interest in the economy, eventhough one single rate of exchange is in operation.

The model creates conditions for financial instability. Banks get trapped between high rates of funding to the domestic market without paying even a real rate of interest on small savings. Given the high volatility they are producing domestic rates of interest have to be kept to high, even if their costs of funding are not so high.

Nevertheless the core of the model is in the relationship that the real and financial sides establish. The problem is that the export leaders are not paying for their bills. The finance of that deficit, the 'private deficit', is carried out by with the operation of the financial sector, which obtains high rates of profit in the short run, but pushes the financial sector to the brink of collapse.

That is why we have to stress that the new model rests on the need of important transfers. The consistency of its 'market orientation', however, is not evident at all. Under conditions of macroeconomic duality, monetary policy becomes meaningless. It cannot properly control the monetary base M, and cannot influence either the rate of interest, or avoid over-exposing the financial sector. The way the model was operated, though successfully bringing Mexico into the world economy, created the conditions for the 1994–95 crisis and its repetition in 1998.

Notes

1. I would like to thank David Barkin, Fernando Noriega and Eduardo Loría for their earlier comments.
2. Sectors are: 1–4, primary; 5–10 extractive; 11–23 foods industry; 24–32 and 59 textiles and light industries; 33–42 chemicals; 43–47 iron ore and other heavy industries; 48–58 and 61 motor cars, motor parts, transport equipment, electronics and electric equipment; 68–72 services; 63–65 hotels and restaurants, 60 construction and 62 retail.
3. See Ortiz (1998) for a detailed presentation on productivity and employment.
4. This fact has been documented by the Central Bank, in its annual reports (Bank of Mexico, Banco de México 1993–95).
5. These, according to NIPA accounts produced by the INEGI, include the subsectors of chemicals and petrochemicals, 33–42, metal, mechanical and transport sectors, 43–47 and 48–58.
6. A proper estimate on real exchange rate for that period is in Morales, (1996).
7. See Krugman (1987).
8. Evidence on this point is presented in Ortiz (1997).
9. Private external debt eventually has to be backed by public resources.
10. Adjusted for the inflation tax and seignorage.
11. The actual rate of growth for 1994 is ambiguous.
12. See 'Informe sobre la situación económica, las finanzas públicas y la deuda pública', primer trimestre de 1995, SHCP.
13. Namely, portfolio and currency substitution approaches. See Pentecost (1993).

References

Bank of Mexico (1997).

Consultoria Internacional Especializada, S.A. de C.V. Mexico *Stata Matrix*, (1990) and (1995).

Cornfold, A. and J. Kregel (1996) 'Globalisation, capital flows and international regulation', The Jerome Levy Economics Institute Working paper, No. 161.
Instituto Nacional de Estadistica Geografia e Informatica (INEGI) *National Income and Product Accounts (NIPA) 1970–1995*.
Krugman, P. (1987) *Rethinking International Trade* (MIT Press).
The Ministry of the Treasury (SHCP) (1997).
Morales, R. (1996) 'Mexico: Valuacion de la Moneda y Sostenibilidad del Tipo de Cambio', *Comercio exterior*. vol. 46, No. 4, pp. 295–307.
Ortiz, E. (1997) 'El cambio estructural en Mexico y las empresas pequeñas y medianas', *Comercio Exterior*, vol. 47, No. 1, pp. 16–26.
Ortiz, E. (1998) 'Déficit Privado e Inestabilidad en la economía Mexicana', *Comercio Exterior*, Vol. 48, No. 6, pp. 461–72.
Pentecost, E. (1993) *Exchange Rate Dynamics* (Edward Elgar).

4 Entrepreneurial strategies in response to structural change in Mexico

Celso Garrido

Within the new economic order, born out of the structural reform carried out in Mexico, there is a small but powerful group of large private Mexican industrial enterprises (hereafter referred to as LPIEs). This group has restructured itself and occupies a leading position with a sustained dynamic expansion at the national and international level (see Table 4.1).

Table 4.1 Ranking of the 37 biggest private businesses in Latin America, 1994 (by order of sales volume, $m)

Ranking	*Sector leader* (L)	*Business*	*Sector*	*Total sales*	*Country*
1	L	Telmex	Telecommunications	8,635.5	Mexico
2	L	Vitro	Glass	4,194.7	Mexico
3		Carso	Tobacco	3,348.1	Mexico
4	L	Cemex	Cement	3,146.6	Mexico
5	L	Visa	Beverages/ beer	2,776.5	Mexico
6	L	Alfa	Steel	2,773.5	Mexico
7		CSN	Steel	2,653.4	Brazil
8		Copersucar	Foodstuffs	2,340.9	Brazil
9		Grupo Acerero del Norte	Steel	2,170.0	Mexico
10	L	Copene	Petrochemicals	2,104.5	Brazil
11		Usiminas	Steel	2,084.7	Brazil
12	L	ICA	Construction	2,048.3	Mexico
13	L	TELEVISA	Tel., radio and pub.	1,904.3	Mexico
14		Modelo	Beverages/ beer	1,878.2	Mexico
15		Brahma	Beverages/ beer	1,870.0	Brazil
16		Bimbo	Foodstuffs	1,795.4	Mexico

Table 4.1 (Contd)

Ranking	*Sector leader* (L)	*Business*	*Sector*	*Total sales*	*Country*
17	L	Desc	Autoparts	1,637.3	Mexico
18		Encol	Construction	1,203.8	Brazil
19		Industrial Minera	Mining	1,148.5	Mexico
20	L	Kimberly-Clark	Paper products	1,146.6	Mexico
21		Celanese	Chemicals	1,075.8	Mexico
22	L	Transportación Marítima, TMM	Maritime transport	1,000.9	Mexico
23		Papeles y Cartones (CMPC)	Paper products	925.3	Chile
24		Grupo Tribasa	Construction	908.6	Mexico
25		Grupo Mexicano de Desarrollo	Construction	898.6	Mexico
26		Cydsa	Petrochemicals	885.5	Mexico
27		Klabin	Paper products	825.1	Brazil
28		Copesul	Petrochemicals	716.9	Brazil
29	L	Sau Paulo Alpargatas	Textiles	644.9	Brazil
30		Suzano	Paper products	622.3	Brazil
31		Sudamericana de Vapores	Maritime transport	589.9	Chile
32		Alpargatas Santista	Textiles	511.8	Brazil
33		Votoramtim	Cement	486.1	Brazil
34		Grupo Synkro	Textiles	479.4	Mexico
35		Pérez Companc	Maritime transport	424.2	Argentina
36		Celbrás	Textiles	378.7	Brazil
37		Folha da Manha	TV, radio and publishing	345.6	Brazil
		37 Businesses	**16 Sectors**	**62,580.4**	**4 countries**

Notes: (L): Indicates that the business is a sales leader within the sample of 500 of Latin America.
Source: based upon *América Economía, Las 500 mayores empresas de América Latina*. Edición 1995–96.

This is noteworthy for the extraordinary changes and challenges that businesses in general faced as a result of the reform, and for the grave economic situation that these large businesses in particular suffered in 1982. The successful evolution of the LPIEs stands out for its marked contrast with the generalised deterioration that the remaining businesses of the country experienced during these years.

Basically, the successful restructuring of the LPIEs was a result of the interaction between three distinct groups of factors. First, the changes in the conditions of competition induced by the government strategy of economic reform and the support that the government gave to these LPIEs to help them to go through their restructuring process. Secondly, the transformations in the patterns of manufacturing specialisation, and the foreign trade of the country. Thirdly, the strategies of restructuring and expansion applied by the LPIEs themselves. Together these created a complex set of interrelations of which, given the limitations of this article, only some of the common features to the strategic responses of the LPIEs will be analysed.[1] The purpose is to assess the mode in which these LPIEs internalized and assess the macroeconomic and sectorial changes with the aforementioned success.

CHALLENGES AND CONDITIONS OF THE STRATEGIES CARRIED OUT BY THE LPIEs

In general, the principal strategic challenges to the LPIEs at the start of the 1990s were the new forms of competition, which emerged as a result of changes in the national and international economic conditions. That is to say, given the processes of deregulation and trade liberalisation, these businesses had to face the modalities of global competition with other national as well as international enterprises. These modalities of competition are not based upon the traditional opposition between internal and external markets, but are a product of a complex interrelation between both, which is subordinated to the global logic and obliges these businesses to consider all levels of action in their strategies.

In the internal market, the new competitive contexts have been present in Mexico since 1989, given the increase in imports stimulated by the opening up of the economy, the overvaluation of the exchange rate, and the demand for low cost inputs. Added to this was the strategic threat of greater direct foreign competition in the country, starting in 1994, with the initiation of NAFTA.

In the international economy, given economic globalisation (Chesnais, 1994), the large transnational oligopolies are the actors that determine the nature of the competition. This is done by integrating in a global logic the productive, commercial and financial processes in the diverse national economies as well as at the international level. With this new transnational oligopolistic competition there is an increase in the concentration of economic power, but this occurs through new modes of organisation under the form of business webs, influenced strongly by the experience of the Japanese firms of the Keiretsu type or 'toyotism'. This form of organisation operates by both externalising its activities and by decentralisation, as well as by internalising externalities and generating quasi-integration.

All of the above takes place on the basis of new dynamic sectors (electronics, information technology, services, and biotechnology) that appear to be displacing traditional industries in the postwar economy. Alongside this, with the rise in capital flows towards developing countries, direct investment on a world scale has taken new directions and characteristics; there appear new expressions of this investment such as fusion, acquisitions, franchises or strategic alliances. Finally, there is a strong channelling of these investments towards services.[2]

In sum, the worldwide competition operates through new systematic interactions between oligopolies, markets, cooperation and the state. With this there is a transformation of both the characteristics of access to markets and potential areas of activity as well as the forms by which barriers, which inhibit access, are created.

SOME COMMONALTIES IN THE STRATEGIES OF THE LPIEs

In general, the LPIEs responded to the new challenges of global competition with complex and novel strategies compared with what had been their former style. The strategies for the seven major private economic groups can be seen in Table 4.2.

A general analysis of these commonalties in the strategies reveals the following. On the one hand, the LPIEs developed cycles of investment in plants and equipment that permitted them to increase their efficiency and productivity in their principal product lines with respect to their foreign competitors. They also achieved standards of quality closer to or equivalent to international levels. This took place along with processes of production re-specialisation on behalf of those conglomerates that formed these LPIEs, selling those businesses which were not priorities for the corporations without, however, abandoning the diversification strategies determined by the dynamic of their business activities. Presently these economic groups are participating actively in the new privatisations (ports, petrochemicals, and railways) as well as the liberalisation of telecommunications.

Table 4.2 Profile of elements in the strategies of seven private national Mexican groups (1983–95)

				Alfa	*Carso*	*Cemex*	*Desc*	*Pulsar*	*Visa*	*Vitro*
Has a financial group	Yes				☒		☒	☒	☒	☒
	No			☒		☒				
Has diversified investments	Yes	Changed portfolio of investments	Yes	☒	☒		☒	☒	☒	
			No							
	No					☒				☒
Internationalised sales	Yes	Foreign sales	> 50 %			☒				
			< 50%	☒	☒		☒	☒	☒	☒
	No									
Property open to the market	Yes			☒	☒	☒	☒	☒	☒	☒
	No									
Growth strategy	Bought businesses	Yes	In the country		☒	☒	☒	☒	☒	
			Abroad	☒		☒		☒	☒	☒
		No								
	Bought public businesses	Yes			☒		☒			
		No		☒		☒		☒	☒	☒
	Invoted in modernisation and new plants		Yes	☒	☒	☒	☒	☒	☒	☒
			No							
	Strategic alliances with foreign businesses		Important	☒	☒	☒	☒		☒	☒
			Occasional					☒		
Reforms the work process	Yes			☒		☒		☒		
	No									
Impact of the present crisis	Favourable					☒				
	Controllable in the short term			☒	☒		☒	☒	☒	☒
	Grave									

Source: Garrido (1995).

On the other hand, the LPIEs continued and deepened the tendency to expand their foreign activities, which initiated in 1983. This tendency was in part an expression of the fact that these businesses needed to expand their markets, given the limited size of the internal market. However, after 1988 this behaviour was combined with the new logic of the global competition which induced these businesses to position themselves in their foreign competitor's markets through direct investments in order to consolidate a stable presence in the said markets. This was related to a significant increase in the scale of the business activity of these LPIEs, fundamentally determined by the privatisations of public enterprises and reinforced by the effects of these trade and investment activities in the foreign markets.

Similarly, it is noteworthy that these businesses have assumed more decentralised forms of organisation and tend to modify their forms of property and control in order to establish new links with foreign capitals, without this meaning the abandonment of the traditional family property structure.

Finally, and in contrast with the above, it should be pointed out that the restructuring and expansion of the LPIEs was carried out without a favourable impact on the rest of the businesses in the country. In fact to benefit from importing more competitive inputs it weakened the client–server relations maintained with these.

On the whole, the strategies of the LPIEs can be summarised in the operation of new combinations of competition and cooperation between the defence of home markets and the conquest of positions in foreign markets, together with new articulations in the relations with the state and with the transnational enterprises.[3]

THE DEFENCE OF THE INTERNAL MARKET

With respect to the internal market, the strategy of the LPIEs was to increase the entrance barriers, which their traditional leadership provided them. The objective was to relatively neutralise the impact of the trade liberalisation and the threats created by opportunities for foreign direct investment in the country as a consequence of the NAFTA. To do this they combined the use of the power they had over those segments of the internal market where they operated with their affinities to political power. Together with this they formed strategic alliances with some of the large foreign enterprises that had intentions of entering to compete in the country, particularly in the generalised consumer goods sectors such as, for example, beer, refreshments and cold cuts. These alliances didn't have an exclusively defensive character. That is, while establishing agreements to distribute the foreign competitor's products in the country, they were habitually combined with agreements so that the products of the Mexican enterprise would be distributed by the competitor's in their own markets or directly empowering the former to do so. Some of the principal alliances that were established up to 1993 are listed in Table 4.3.

The novelty of these alliances doesn't permit definite conclusions with respect to the results these have over the LPIEs, but it is evident that they can be ephemeral at both the national and international levels, as is illustrated by example of the Vitro-Carning Inc. experience.

Another line of action that was followed in order to increase the entrance barriers was to generate relatively high supply levels with respect to the size of the internal market, with the aim of discouraging possible new competitors. That was achieved by increasing the 'preventive' investments in the country and through acquisitions and fusion with other local enterprises. This last type of response was particularly important in cases such as that of cement, where the struggle for the internal market fits into a broader competition with the big transnationals in the world market.

Additionally, it can be seen that one of the responses of the LPIEs was the attempt to modernise the entrepreneurial perspectives with respect to total quality, and to the orientation of promotions to the consumer. This has implied important reorganisation and training efforts in the businesses and changes in the social valorisation of the entrepreneurial attitudes. However, up to now there is not much evidence of the effects of these efforts, beyond that of paying homage to an expression of the new age.

Another important factor in the increase of entrance barriers was the factual agreement between the LPIEs and the government, by which only private Mexican enterprises could participate in the privatisation of the large public enterprises. This was significant for parts of the industrial sector, for example, the steel mills, fertiliser plants, mines, corn mills and sugar refineries, and even telecommunications. In Table 4.4 information on some of the large privatisations carried out during the administration of Salinas de Gortari is presented.

This restriction on foreign investment permitted the LPIEs to accede to more profitable business areas. At the same time, as was mentioned before, it increased the scale of their activity very

Table 4.3 Associations and shared investments between Mexican and foreign businesses

Mexican business	*Foreign business*	*Description*
Alfa	Grupo Metecno Spa	Dedicated to the fabrication of isolated panels in the construction industry (Italy) Capital: $20 million
Alfa – Celanese	Eastman–Kodak (US)	Trade in polyester. Capital: $300 million
Tamsa	Siderca (Argentina)	The association involves capitalising the Mexican business with $75 million
Vitro	Pilkington Bros (GB)	The Mexican business Corning signed agreements to produce and sell articles of glass and crystal
Vitro	Whirlpool American	Joint participation in electrodomestics and appliances
Vitro	Corning Inc. (US)	**Cinfurar** a worldwide company to produce kitchen and table articles.
Cydsa	Jansen (US)	Association to facilitate the sale of fibres in the US
Cydsa	Veratec (US)	The business Bonlam (Grupo Cydsa) established an agreement to distribute non-sewed fibre products in Mexico and Central America.
Automotríz Dina	Navistar (US)	7.4 per cent of Dina Camiones is foreign-owned.
Spicer	GKN (US)	GKN increased its participation in Velcon from 25 per cent to 39 per cent.
Bimbo	Sara Lee (US)	Association to facilitate the distribution of Mexican products in the United States
Sigma Alimentos	Oscar Meyer Foods (US)	The affiliate of the Alfa group and the business Phillip Morris will build a milk products plant in Mexico.
Geupec	Pepsico Inc. (US)	Pepsico bought 28.9 per cent of Geusa, and announced that together with Geupec, Protexa and Envasa will invest $750 million in the sale of soft drinks.
Femsa refrescos	Coca Cola Co.	Femsa sold 30 per cent of its soft drink division to Coca Cola for $195 million Coca Cola (United States) announced additional investments for $500 million.
GGemex	Natural Beverage (Canada)	Grupo Embotellador Mexicano will distribute the product line Clearly Canadian.
Modelo	Anheuser Busch (US)	The American firm acquired 17.7 per cent of the Mexican brewery for $400 million.

Source: *El Financiero*, various issues.

Table 4.4 Selected privatisations of non-financial public enterprises during the salinas de gortari administration

	Company	*Date of sale*	*Purchaser*	*Activity*	*Bid*
1	Telefonos de Mexico	13 Dec. 1990	Grupo Carso, S.W. Bell, France Cable and Radio	Telecommunications	1,760.0
2	Cananea Mining Co.	28 Sept. 1990	Mexicana de Cananea	Copper mine	475.0
3	Aeronaves de Mexico	12 June 1989	Icaro Aerotransportes	Airline	268.0
4	Mexicana de Aviacion	22 Aug. 1989	Grupo Xabre	Airline	140.0
5	Fomento Azucarero	13 Jan. 1989	Grupo Beta San Miguel	Sugar refinery	89.0
6	Conasupo, Tutitlan plant	23 Feb. 1990	Unilever	Vegetable oils and seeds	74.5
7	Grupo Diana	27 Oct. 1989	Consorcio 'G' (Cummins)	Tractors, buses and motors	56.0
8	Sugar refineries	1 Oct. 1990	Corp. Indus. Sucrum	Sugar refineries	54.5
9	Mexinox	23 Mar. 1990	Ahorrinox	Iron and steel	47.6
10	Sugar refineries	19 June 1990	Anermmex	Sugary refinery	42.6
11	Group of television channels, cinemas and film studios		Radio television broadcast centre	Communications	680.0
12	Miconsa	3 Oct. 1993	Fideicomiso Molinero Promotora Empresarial	Corn for industrial use	140.0

Note: In millions of dollars. The conversion to dollars was made using the exchange rate for the date of the auction.
Sources: *El Financiero*, Mexican Newspaper, various issues.

significantly, which in several cases approximated their size to that of the giant conglomerates.

A second dimension where the privatisations had an extraordinary impact on the economical power and institutional structure of the LPIEs was the privatisation of the banks and the formation of industrial–financial groups (see Table 4.5).

This type of group had already existed before the 1982 crisis, but had been eliminated by the nationalisation of the commercial banks that was carried out in that year. With the bank reforms of 1990, financial groups were authorised, and although the connections of these with the industrial enterprises were prohibited, these were in fact tolerated, giving rise to the aforementioned industrial–financial groups.

According to the available evidence, the LPIEs that integrated into these financial groups gained extraordinary benefits over their competitors, both due to their participation in the very high profits of the banks between 1990 and 1993 and to the advantages of the access to credit in the international markets.

Since the end of 1994, this industrial–financial link began to have an unforeseen negative counterpart, as the bankruptcy of the banks meant that these groups had to absorb the heavy financial burden that had resulted.[4] In some cases, such as the example of the Vitro group, which is the controller of the financial group Serfin, the problems of the latter provoked the industrial group into capitalising the financial segment. This has negatively affected the investment plans of the industrial segment. However, in general the LPIEs affiliated to the financial–industrial groups have maintained their expansionary dynamic on the basis of the activities that they have developed in the foreign markets, at the same time as they were trying to isolate the unfavourable evolution of their financial segment.[5]

Some public policies also had favourable effects over the empowerment of the leadership of the LPIEs in the internal market, particularly in the fiscal area, and in the foreign trade and political sectors.

For example, in fiscal matters the directors of the private tabacco duopoly (Cigatam/Grupo CARSO and the Moderna/Grupo Pulsar) negotiated a tax reduction without the corresponding obligation to reduce sale prices to the public. With this the enterprises belonging to these groups achieved a notable increase in their cash flow, which substantially improved their financial capacity and permitted them to expand to other activities by buying, fusing with, or creating businesses.[6]

In the realm of sectorial policies, particularly important were those applied in the case of the programs to expand highways and bridges,

Table 4.5 Principal private national financial–economic groups distinguishing between 'traditional' and 'new' (formed during the salinas de gortari administration)

Type	*Group name*	*Financial institution*	*Industry*	*Trade/services*
Traditional	Visa	Bancomer	Beer	
	Vitro	Serfin – Obsa	Glass	
	Desc	Mexicano – Invermexico	Petrochemical/foodstuffs	
New	Carso	Inbursa	Tabacco/telephones/mining Autoparts/ construc. mat.	Department stores
	Hermes	Interacciones	Transportations – trucks	
	Maseca	Banorte	Agroindustry	
	Alcantara	Bancrecer/ Banoro	Transport	
	Pulsar	Seguros la Republica	Tobacco/agroindustry	
	Prime	Internacional – Prime	Beer	

Source: based upon hemerographical information and documentation.

which bolstered the market for the cement producers and the building companies. This same orientation motivated the decision of the government to deregulate the production of nixtamal, which is a product of popular consumption, traditionally regulated by law. The government allowed the MASECA and MINSA groups to produce it, given their more advanced technology and provided them with the government subsidies, which allowed them to maintain low costs, to displace the small family owned mills.

Finally, within the same context it is also pertinent to refer to the already mentioned NAFTA negotiations. In these negotiations the LPIEs were leaders of the inter-sectorial and institutional commission that was formed for the same purpose, denominated COECE for its initials in Spanish. This permitted them to fight to prolong the barriers to foreign capital to the longest period possible, at the same time as they sought to gain positions in the other two national markets.

INTERNATIONALISATION OF THE BUSINESSES AND FOREIGN POSITIONING

The other major area of strategies followed by the LPIEs to consolidate their leadership was to internationalise their businesses and position themselves in the foreign markets to consolidate their perspectives in the global competition.

The LPIEs successfully fulfilled this exporting evolution after 1988, while preserving their power over the internal market. This was achieved by increasing their share in the already mentioned cycle of investments, and installing capacity to consolidate the turn towards exporting at the same time as they continued satisfying their internal demand. The maintenance of these export positions under distinct macroeconomic and exchange rate contexts, such as those registered in the country since then, indicates that this export behaviour responds to forces which are endogenous to the same sectors and businesses. However, it's necessary to recall that, as with the rest of the large Latin American businesses, these firms export products that are relatively backward with respect to the dynamic of world trade, such as some basic inputs (cement, glass, steel) or mass consumer goods (beer, foodstuffs).

A relevant aspect of this evolution in the foreign trade of the LPIEs is the new character acquired by these businesses' imports. As is known, the government's liberalisation strategy combined the promotion of exports with a stimulus for temporary imports of inputs for products that would be exported. This had the aim of stimulating the competitiveness of the exporters, given that it put them in conditions of international competition with regards to the cost and quality of their inputs. However, the former seems to have had an adverse effect over the linkage of the LPIE exporters with their national suppliers, as these links had been weakened due to the attractiveness offered by foreign suppliers. This was what was on the mind of one director of these large industrial groups when he expressed in an interview that, from his point of view, a global business was one 'that bought where it was advantageous, produced where it was advantageous, and sold where it was advantageous'. Consequently, the export strategy followed by the LPIEs was unfavourable for the local producers with respect to the client–supplier links, although this was also determined by the weak and inadequate supply capacity of said producers.

Together with their export activities, various LPIEs invested directly in the external markets to position themselves in their competitors' markets or to build the global production nets as required by the particular mode of globalisation of the industries where they operated. This strategy of internationalisation with foreign direct investment was primarily expressed in the purchase or fusion of already existing businesses. It was vital for these investments that the LPIEs could obtain access to financing in the New York stock market or in the Euromarket, as successfully occurred since 1990.

The internationalisation via direct investment had diverse effects. On the one hand, it meant creating a balance between the production for domestic use, and for exports. The result of this was realised by Mexican businesses as never seen before. This, however, had diverse effects for the course of the crisis that began in December of 1994. On the other hand, this internationalisation also implied the necessity of opening up these Mexican businesses to foreign capital. In some cases, this meant changing their corporate structure to assure greater autonomy and decentralization of the divisions according to the specific modalities demanded by the markets where they operated.

CONCLUSION

In conclusion we highlight two relevant problems that occurred as a result of the grand strategic alignments held in common by the LPIEs. To do this we will make use of the elements provided by the typology of the principal LPIEs in Mexico as shown in Table 4.6.

Table 4.6 Typology of large private national industry enterprises (April 1997)

Type of enterprises			*Name of conglomerate*	*Name of business*	*Industrial branch*	*With foreign businesses*	*Exports*
	with bank	traditional	Visa	Visa–Femsa	Drinks	X	X
				Unicom–GGTE	Telephone service		
		new	Grupo Maseca	Gruma	Corn products	X	X
		traditional		Cemex	Cement	X	X
				Kimberly Clark	Paper		
				Crisoba	Paper		
				Televisa	TV. radio and publishing	X	X
				Modelo	Beer		X
				Bimbo	Bread	X	X
Integrated around a product line	without bank			GIMM	Mining		X
				TMM	Transport		X
				IMSA	Steel	X	X
				GMD	Construction		
				Peñoles	Mining		X
				GEM	Drinks		
				Continental	Drinks		
				Synkro	Textiles		X
				Ramirez	Autoparts		X
				Cummings	Autoparts		X
				Fresnillo	Mining		X
		new		GAN–AHMSA	Steel		X
				Tribasa	Construction		
Diversified	with bank	traditional	Desc	Agrobios	Foodstuffs		
				Unik	Autoparts		X
				IRSA	Chemical		
			Vitro	Vitro	Glass	X	X

				Vitro–Whirpool	Electrodomestic		X
		new	Carso	Telmex	Telephone services	X	
				Cigatam	Tobacco		
				Condumex	Electrical		X
				Nacobre	Metallurgy		X
				Euzkadi–'G' Tire	Rubber		X
				Frisco	Mining		X
			Pulsar	La Moderna	Tobacco	X	X
				Ponderosa	Paper		X
	without bank	traditional	Alfa	Sigma	Foodstuffs	X	
				Hylsamex	Steel		X
				Alpek	Chemical		X
				Petrocel	Petrochemical		
				Alestra–ATT	Telephone service		
			Iusacel	IUSACEL	Telephone service		
			ICA	ICA	Construction	X	X
Financial–industrial	financial group	new	Banamex–Accival	Avantel–MCI	Telephone service		

Source: based upon hemerographical data and documents.

The first problem refers to the limited reach that this reorientation of the LPIEs has had with respect to their productive orientation as well as to their relation with the global economy. With respect to the limits of the restructuring, we have seen that while the LPIEs realised an important investment cycle, this was carried out to improve their traditional product lines. These products are relatively mature and face extraordinary competition at a world level. That is why they offer limited prospects for the assurance of the long-term dynamism of the economy. With regards to the level of insertion of these LPIEs in the global economy it must be pointed out that, as can be noted in Table 5.6, only a limited number of these have succeeded in adequately combining the organisational and productive changes that was required to face the new competition, with the exploitation of the relative advantages derived from their positions of leadership in the internal market. In other words, only few LPIEs managed to establish new articulations between exports and foreign direct investment. For this reduced group, their old protected internal market is now only part of their global business map. Such is the case, for example, of Cementos Mexicanos (CEMEX), of which Mexico is now a division within the North American region. The great majority of the LPIEs continue to have their principal support in the internal market, although they have had success in the foreign markets, due to substantial change in the balance between national and international markets for Mexico.

This brings us to the second major problem that this new profile of the LPIEs presents for the country. The fact that this evolution of the LPIEs is accompanied by poor linkages with the rest of the national businesses continues to be a grave limitation for the transmission of the dynamism of these businesses to the rest of the economy. On the whole, the problems highlighted indicate that in order to maintain a long-term dynamic these LPIEs should adopt a change in their investment areas, towards the more dynamic industries in the global economy, which includes a change of mentality with respect to innovation and scientific technological development. Together with this, as a condition of systemic competitiveness, they should actively contribute to develop business nets that consolidate a powerful entrepreneurial fabric in the country. This assumes changes in the focus of the country's industrial policy so that the country develops state activities equivalent to those developed by the states of more successful foreign competitors.

Notes

1. It is well known that there are diverse methods for analysing the competitive strategies (Porter, 1986, 1987; Chesnais, 1994; and Dickens, 1992. Similarly, it is important to point out the differences in the strategic responses that have been taken by distinct businesses in Mexico. On this point an example can be found in Ramirez and Unger (1996), and Garrido (1995, 1997b).
2. See World Bank (1997).
3. Paraphrasing Fruin (1994), we could say that the case of the structural reform and configuration of a new entrepreneurial leadership in Mexico has common features with the Japanese experience: 'a model of institutional development under the conditions of late economic development and the predomination of private initiative that ends up some place between the development of state capitalism and a free market economy'. The comparison is valid only when taking into account the substantive differences that distinguish both experiences.
4. For an analysis of the banking crisis and its impact over financial power in the country, please see Garrido (1997a).
5. It is notorious that this result is related to the extraordinary governmental programmes for the rescue of the banks – extraordinary for the impressive quantities involved (see Garrido, 1997a). Similarly, it is valid to point out that this evolution of the Mexican industrial–financial groups confirms what Singh(1992) had indicated with respect to the Latin American case. The control structure of these groups operates contrary to the manner indicated by Aoki and Patrick (1994) for the Japanese case, given that here the industrial segment dominates the financial one.
6. Both are found among the 'new' groups, given that they were recently created in the 1980s.

References

América Economia, *500 mayores empresas de América Latina. 1995–96* edition.

Aoki, Mashiko and Patrick, Hugh (1994) *The Japanese Main Banking System*, Oxford University Press, New York.

Chesnais, François (1994) *La Mondialisation de Capital*, Syros, Paris.

Dickens Peter (1992) *Global Shift. The Internationalisation of Economic Activity*, Guilford Press, New York.

El Financiero, various issues.

Fruin, Mark, W. (1994) *The Japanese Enterprise System*, Clarendon Paperbacks, Oxford, England.

Garrido, Celso (1995) *Estrategias económicas de siete grupos privados nacionales en México 1983–1994*, Documento de Investigación elaborado para la Unidad Conjunta CEPAL/ONUDI de Desarrollo Industrial y Tecnológico, Santiago, Chile.

Garrido, Celso (1997a) *Actor bancario y ponder financiero en México. Incertidumbres y desafíos para la nación* in Esthela Gutiérrez Garza (ed.), *El Debate naciona*, vol. 4 (UNAM-U.de Nuevo León).

Garrido, Celso (1997b) *Las grandes empresas industriales privadas en México durante los noventa* in C. Garrido y W. Peres (ed.), *Los grandes grupos industriales privados en América Latina durante los noventa* (UAM-Cepal).
Porter, Michael (ed.), (1986) *Competition in Global Industries* (Boston, Mass.: Harvard Business School Press).
Porter, Michael (1987) *Estrategias competitivas*, México, CECSA.
Ramírez, José Carlos and Unger Kurt (1996) *Las grandes industrias ante la reestructuración: Una evaluación de las estrategias competitivas de las empresas líderes en México*, Documento de trabajo No. 53, División de Economía, CIDE, México.
Singh, Ajit (1992) *The Stock Market and Economic Development: Should Developing Countries Encourage Stocks Markets?*, UNCTAD Discussion papers No 49, Switzerland.
World Bank (1997) *Emerging Markets Facts*, Washington, World Bank.

5 Macroeconomic management under the increasing capital market integration in the Asia–Pacific region: beyond the Tom-Yam effect[1]

Akira Kohsaka

The Asian *currency* crisis that began in mid-1997 has grown into the Asian *economic* crisis. In addition to its serious impact on Asia, the crisis appears to threaten the global economy with the possibility of a world depression. Looking backward, some economists assert that the crisis resulted not primarily from macroeconomic imbalances but from weaknesses in financial systems and governance of corporate as well as government sectors in the crisis economies. Looking forward, some economists criticise that the crisis management so far is not only inadequate but also aggravates the difficulties. We would argue against the former view, and for the latter view in what follows.

This chapter does not intend to test statistically any empirical hypotheses that will be extended there. Rather, it will re-examine conceptual frameworks, based on which policy strategies are constructed, and will give some insights that will hopefully shed some new lights on pre- and in-crisis policy-management issues. We would like to discuss policy implications from the Asian currency crisis in the context of increasing integration of the international capital market not only for emerging market economies but also for the international monetary system. We are presuming that issues at hand for individual emerging markets are how to come to terms with the global capital market, and those for the global economy are how to tame the market.

In the following, we will review the developments in the background of the recent currency crises, particularly increased involvement of emerging markets in the global capital flow (Section I), examine its impacts on macro-monetary management in Thailand (Section II), and discuss what is new and what is not new in various aspects of the Asian currency crisis (Section III). We will see that the currency crisis in Thailand was a typical one, where many of the same forces were at work in different crises, especially under the combination of inflexible exchange rates, domestic financial liberalisation and increased access to the international capital market. Nevertheless, we will argue that both the degree and the scope of contagious results (what we call the Tom-Yam effect) are unproportionately larger than the incipient imbalances of macroeconomic fundamentals.

Then, we will turn to three aspects of policy issues, namely, what was wrong with macroeconomic management in the pre-crisis period (Section IV), then, the present crisis management (Section V) and finally, the global systemic risk management (Section VI). We will argue as follows. First, in the increasingly integrated international capital market, small open economies must learn how to balance between exchange rate stability and foreign capital mobility, even though the scope of their discretion is naturally limited. Secondly, in those highly leveraged economies as East Asia, deflationary policy programmes against the present twin crisis are detrimental to a recovery of confidence in the financial system as well as that of real economic growth. Furthermore, in the short run rehabilitation programmes for crisis management structural reforms should be separated out in order to avoid its negative impact on market expectations for timely recoveries. Thirdly, the present crisis exposed not only the vulnerability of emerging markets' financial system but also that of the international financial system, the latter of which must also be restructured to be ready for unavoidable market failures.

I BACKGROUND OF THE ASIAN CURRENCY CRISIS

In order to discuss the recent Asian currency crisis we must note the role of a huge capital inflow to emerging markets beginning around 1990 (see Figure 5.1). This supported business booms in host economies and led to cause excessive fundamental disequilibrium in goods and/or assets markets, and then its reversal triggered the crisis. Private capital constituted the dominant part of the flow and its size in emerging markets in Asia and Latin America increased from the annual average of $13 billion in the 1980s to $150 billion in 1996, which was larger than the total flows in the 1980s (BIS, 1998).[2]

Figure 5.1a Long-term capital flows: East Asia and Pacific (current US$)

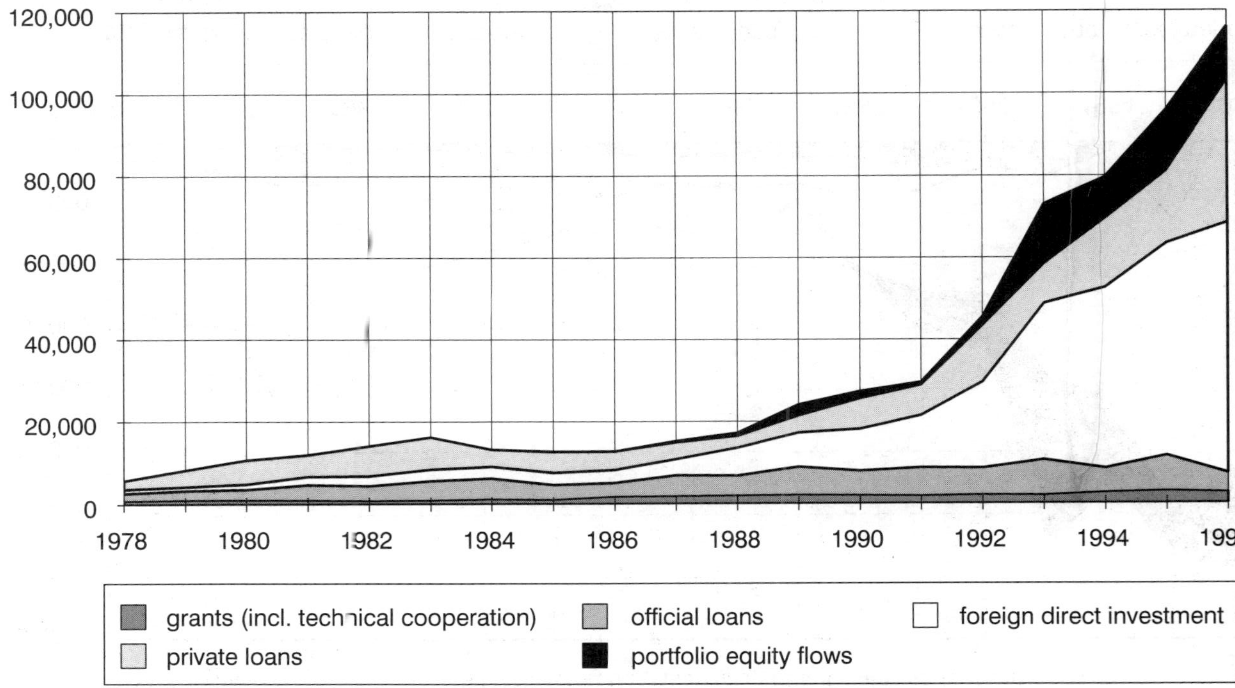

Figure 5.1b Long-term capital flows: Latin America and the Caribbean (current US$)

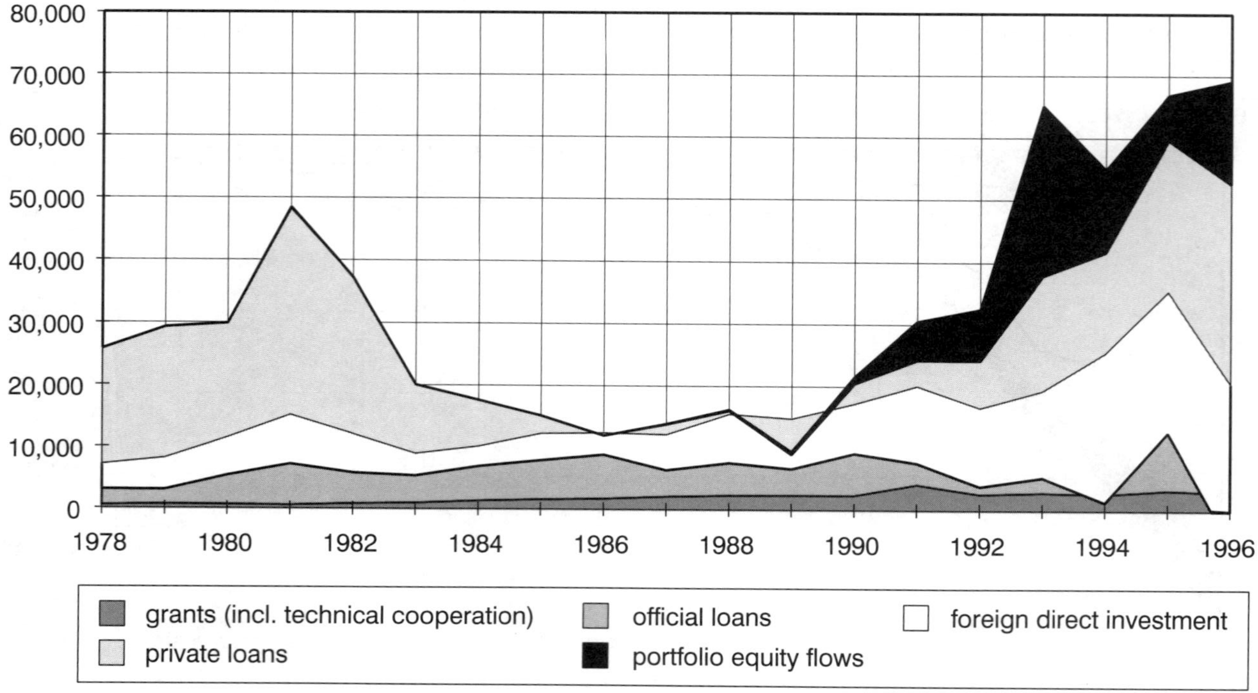

Figure 5.2 Exchange rates and foreign exchange reserves: Thailand

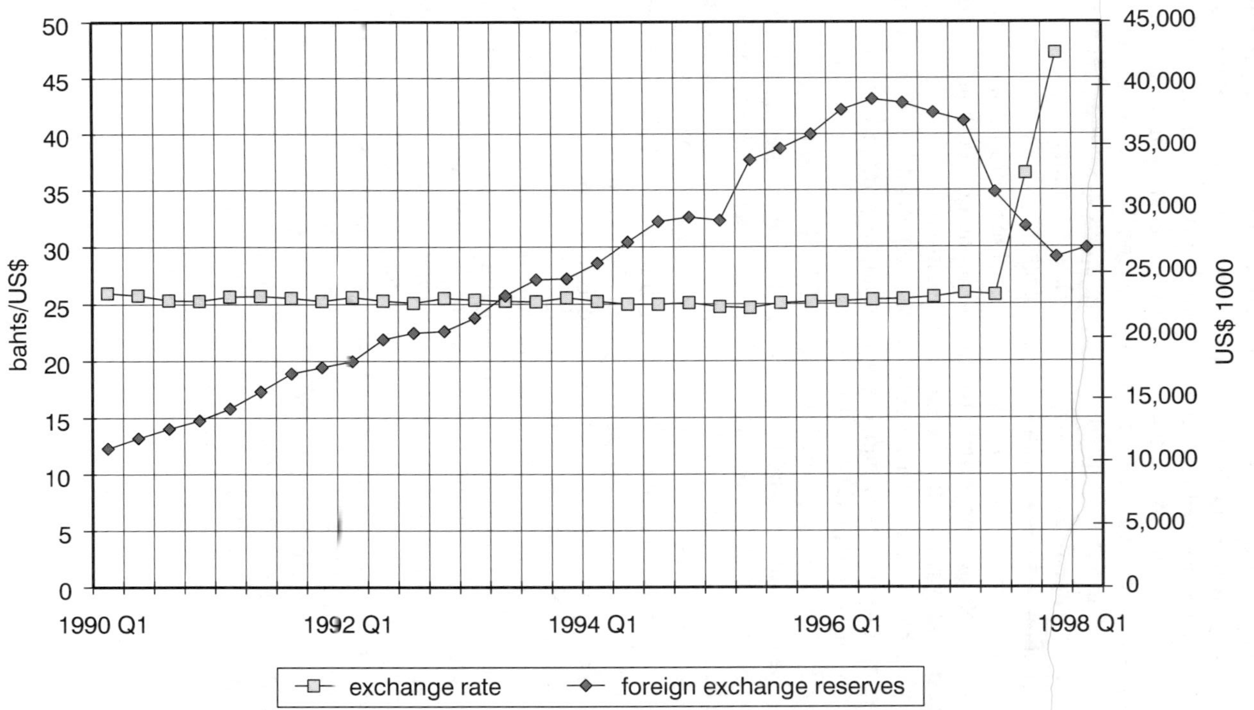

10:17amPart of the reasons for this also exists in developed economies. One is cyclical, namely, once recessions result in a lax demand for funds, investors seek higher returns abroad, including emerging markets, than in home markets. Another is structural, that is, such factors as the securitisation trend since the 1980s, the growth of institutional investors and deregulation measures, and technological advances in finance supporting these trends have activated international divers- ification of financial investments. Another part, of course, exists in emerging markets, which enjoyed favourable assessment of their potential growth and made efforts to attract foreign investment with capital account deregulation.

A currency crisis can be defined as a combination of an acute reduction of foreign exchange reserves and a sudden currency depreciation as in Thailand in 1997 (Figure 5.2). Two features are to be noted. First, a nominal exchange rate of the Thai bahts to the US dollar had been mostly constant at the level of 25 bahts per dollar since the devaluation in 1984 (the virtual US dollar-peg), and, secondly, foreign exchange reserves showed an apparent upward trend in months of imports. In other words, the virtual dollar-peg in Thailand was supported by foreign exchange market intervention with dollar purchases.

A currency crisis is triggered by a sudden reduction or a reversal of foreign capital flows driven by depreciation expectations of currency value becoming dominant. What factors, then, make such depreciation expectations dominant? Deterioration in macroeconomic fundamentals, revealing vulnerabilities in microeconomic structures and self-fulfilling expectations have been cited as the candidates. Which was dominant, then, in the case of the Asian crisis? Noting that *macroeconomic fundamentals and microeconomic structures would not deteriorate overnight*, we must explain how market expectations are formed or at least how they change. Indeed, while currency crises spread to the neighbouring economies like wild fire (*contagion*), no economic forecasts nor credit ratings predicted the crisis ahead, and no asset prices demonstrated its symptoms.[3] Nevertheless, a sudden change in market expectations triggers a currency crisis, which is the very situation that they are afraid of.

II WHAT HAPPENED IN THE TEQUILA AND TOM-YAM EFFECTS?

This is the second time in the 1990s that a contagion of a currency crisis among emerging markets has been witnessed since the Mexican crisis in 1994, when East Asia was said to be not that much affected because they had fewer problems in macroeconomic fundamentals. What was the difference between the two crises? Sachs *et al.* (1996), for example, claim that Mexico had significantly larger macroeconomic fundamental disequilibrium than other emerging markets, while Argentina and Brazil, both seriously affected by the Tequila effect, came next. In fact, prior to the end of 1994, macroeconomic imbalances in terms of real exchange appreciation, domestic credit expansion and foreign exchange reserve adequacy were significantly larger in these three economies than other emerging markets including East Asia (Table 5.1)

The monetary authorities in Thailand began to defend the baht in 1996. In the early 1990s, Thailand switched its financial market policy from conservative gradualism to progressive activism in order to be a financial centre in the Indochina regional development. As a result of active deregulation in capital account transactions, capital inflow to Thailand became as large as 10 per cent of GDP (annual average) in the first half of the 1990s, of which loans (of which one half was short-term) and portfolio flows dominated foreign direct investment.[4] Figure 5.3 shows developments of capital as well as current accounts of

Table 5.1 Mexican currency crisis and financial indicators (%)

Country	*Crisis index*[(a)]	*Real depreciation*[(b)]	*Lending boom*[(c)]	*Reserves adequacy*[(d)]
Indonesia	1.3	11.8	0.7	4.6
Korea	−3.7	−10.3	8.4	6.5
Malaysia	−2.6	9.8	4.0	2.1
Philippines	7.2	−6.7	50.0	4.1
Taiwan	4.4	16.2	46.0	4.7
Thailand	−1.8	0.2	39.2	3.7
Argentina	20.2	−48.0	57.1	3.6
Brazil	17.7	−29.6	−68.3	3.6
Chile	−5.7	−7.5	13.3	1.4
Mexico	79.1	−28.5	116.2	9.1

Note:
[a] a weighted average of nominal depreciation and forex reserve reduction between Nov. 1994 and Apr. 1995; [b] depreciation of real effective exchange rates between 1986–89 and 1990–94; [c] growth rates of ratio of Bank claims on private sector to GDP during 1990–94; [d] ratio of M2 to foreign exchange reserve in Nov. 1994.
Source: Sachs *et al.* (1996).

Figure 5.3 Capital inflows and current accounts: Thailand

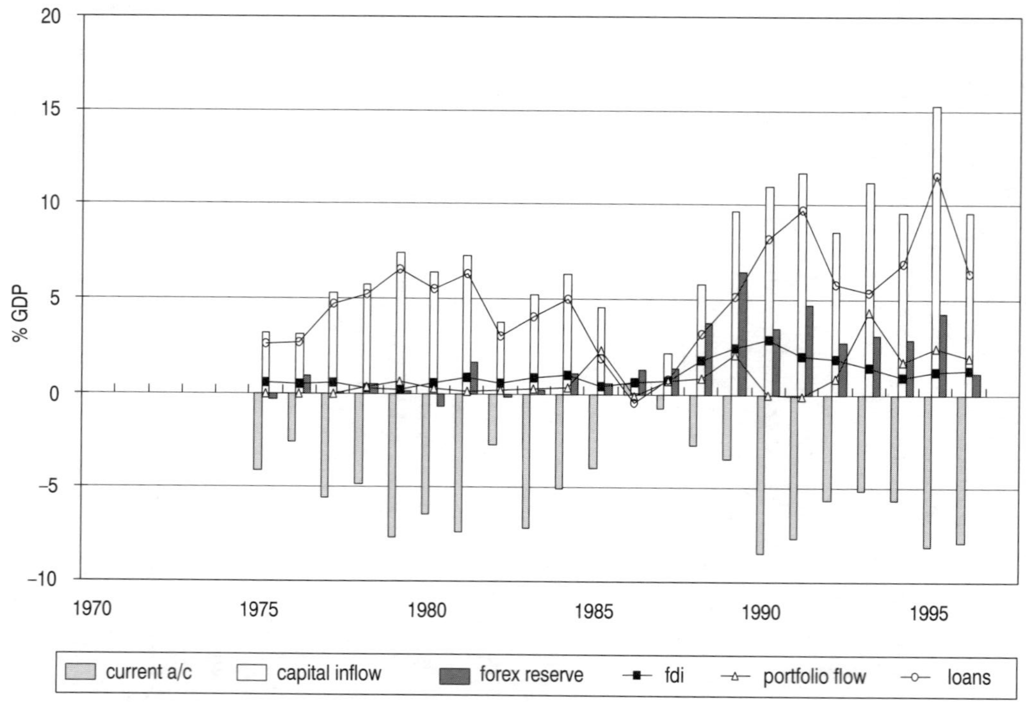

Thailand since the 1970s onward. Meanwhile, a high economic growth since the late 1980s brought about an investment boom with a current account deficit reaching 8 per cent of GDP. With capital account surplus overwhelming current account deficit, the authorities had to prevent the baht from appreciating, thereby accumulating foreign exchange reserves.

Since the foreign exchange market intervention with dollar purchase/ bahts sale is equal to supplying domestic currency, this could have had an expansionary and inflationary effect. So the authorities tried to sterilise any impact of the intervention on domestic currency supply by increasing government deposits from its budget surplus, strengthening the capital of the central bank, and issuing a large amount of central bank bonds. Indeed, when we look at developments in foreign exchange reserves and a monetary base (Figure 5.4), fluctuations in the former were not much reflected in the latter. Thus sterilisation policy seemed to have been successful.

Moreover, when we look at movements of a monetary base (Figure 5.4) and a money supply (Figure 5.5), their growth were not very high, which appeared to suggest that the investment boom was not due to expansionary monetary policy. However, this sterilisation increased domestic interest rates and promoted further capital inflows (mostly, loans) with large interest rate differentials between domestic and offshore markets. A significant part of these loans were short-term loans from off-shore markets by banks and non-bank financial institutions, which were not counted as money supply.

As a matter of fact, these foreign loans played an important leverage role in providing domestic credits. In order to respond to increasing domestic credit needs, those financial institutions borrowed directly from offshore and re lent to domestic investors beyond its resources (i.e. deposits). Just like this, as Figure 5.5 shows, increases in domestic credits as a percentage of GDP were 10 to 15 per cent larger than those in the money supply, thereby sustaining the investment boom. Under high interest rates, significant part of the credits went for investment opportunities with high risk and high return, such as corporate stocks and real estates.

In 1995, despite (or because of) the Tequila effect, Thailand became the largest borrower of bank loans ($39 billion in flow terms) in developing economies, exceeding Korea ($22.5 billion) according to BIS [1997]. However, as a result of US dollar appreciation and export stagnation in the latter half of the year, stock prices levelled off and it became apparent that the bubble had burst. In 1996, the government

Figure 5.4 Foreign exchange reserves and monetary base: Thailand (changes as % of GDP)

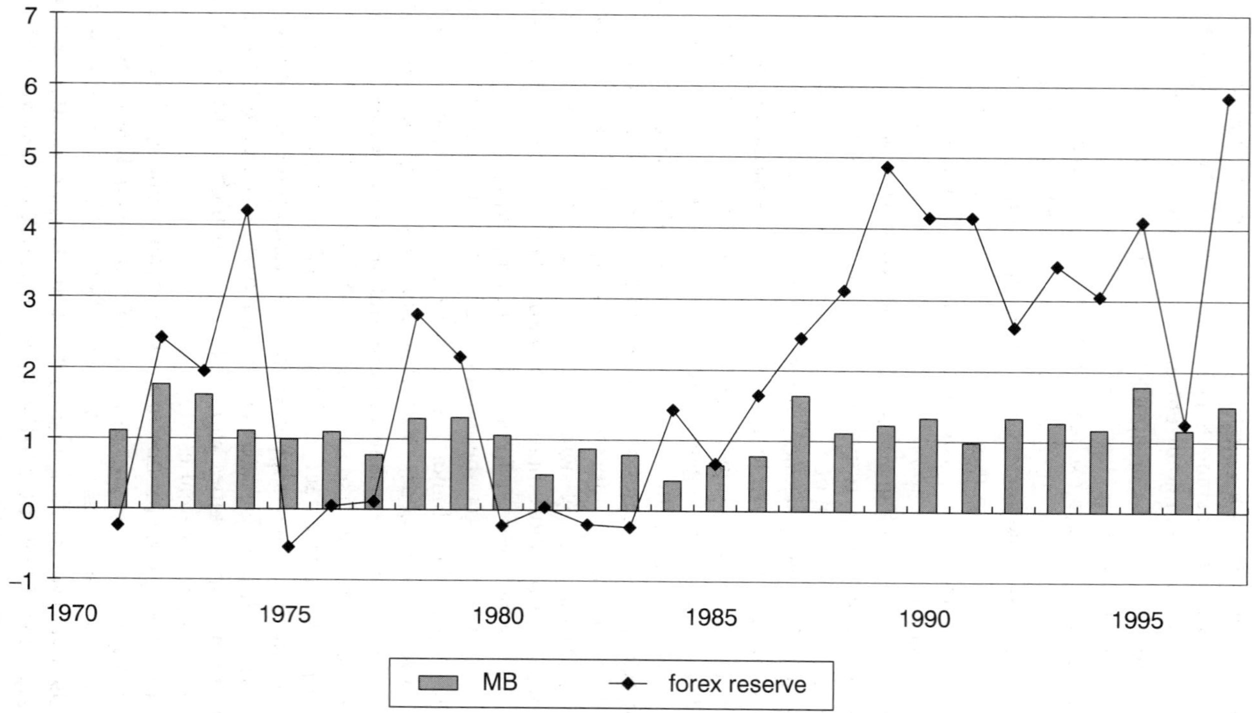

Figure 5.5 Money and credit growth: Thailand(%)

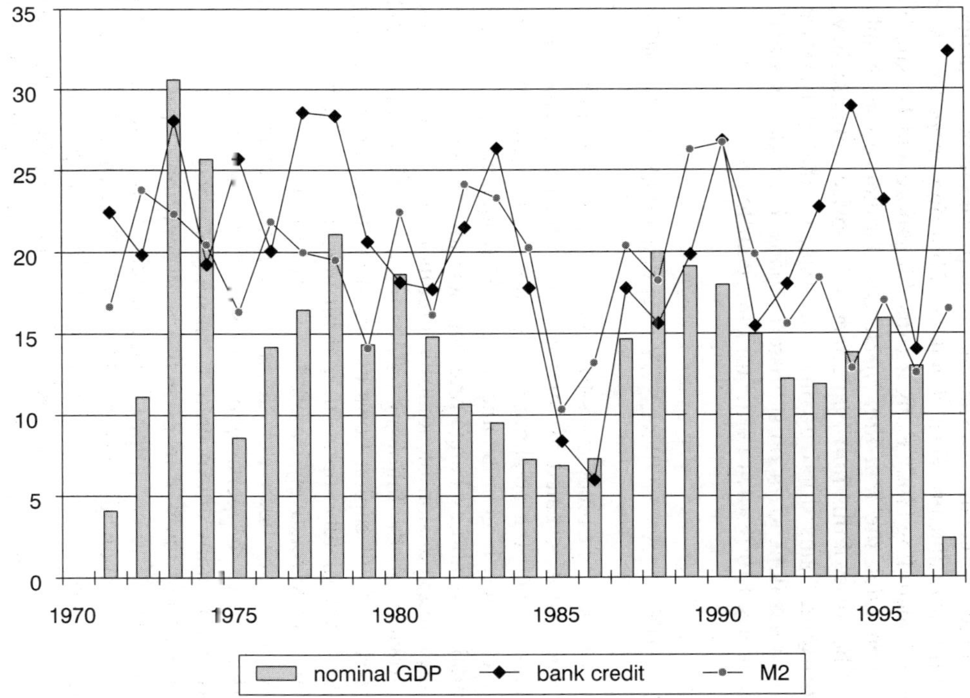

restricted foreign capital flows, but this just aggravated a downward spiral, resulting in increases in bankruptcies of firms and non-performing assets of financial institutions. Capital inflow shrank and the authorities were forced to fend off a series of speculative currency attacks until they gave up the virtual dollar peg in July 1997.

A huge depreciation of the Thai baht proved to be contagious as far as currency values of East Asian neighbouring economies were concerned, including Hong Kong, Korea, Singapore and Taiwan. If we call this contagion the *Tom-Yam effect*, as a parallel to the Tequila effect, then because of this *Tom-Yam* effect, stock prices immediately fell and short-term loans dried up in East Asia, so that particularly those economies dependent on short-term loans, i.e. Indonesia and Korea, were forced to resort to IMF for emergent loans.

III THE ASIAN CURRENCY CRISIS: WHAT IS NEW?

The Mexican currency crisis took place as a rebound of international interest rates revealed its internal and external macroeconomic imbalances,[5] and the neighbouring region, particularly those economies with relatively large imbalances, suffered from a concurrent reversal of capital flows and exchange rate depreciation. In the case of the Asian crisis, overexpansion of domestic credits due to excessive short-term borrowing and the following bubble burst and financial instability led to a reversal of capital flows based on shifts of market expectations, which immediately spread to and hit neighbouring economies, particularly those relatively exposed to short-term loans.

As Asia had been well known as a region of superior economic performance, the persistence and scope of the *Tom-Yam* effect may have been totally unexpected. Even so, this type of crisis is not totally new. Rather, many of its aspects are a repetition of past experiences, where Asia is no exception. First, financial or banking crises occurred more often than not in the 1980s and 1990s with overexpansion of domestic credits prior to crises in both developed and developing economies (see Caprio and Klingebiel (1997), for example). Secondly, simultaneous banking as well as currency crises, or a twin crisis was neither rare nor new. The Chilean experience in the early 1980s has been known as a result of a wrong combination of pegged exchange rates and internal as well as external capital market liberalization.

It is true in the case of Thailand that its persistent external imbalance should have been corrected sooner, but other macroeconomic indicators such as domestic inflation, budget balances and real exchange rates did not necessarily suggest imbalances. As Table 5.2 shows, macroeconomic fundamentals before the Asian currency crisis were far less problematic even in Indonesia, Korea and Malaysia than in Thailand. Nevertheless, all the currencies in East Asia were exposed to speculative currency attacks. They hit even Singapore and Taiwan, which had no hint of macroeconomic troubles, except that their growth expectations might suffer from their close links to those affected economies through trade and investment flows, which we would like to call (negative) *regional externalities*.

One note might be necessary in contrasting the Mexico and Thailand cases. Overconsumption (Mexico) versus overinvestment (Thailand) are sometimes cited as possible reasons for the differences between the two cases (IMF, 1997, for example). We must, however, know that using aggregate figures might conceal one common factor. Namely, as far as national account data is concerned, we can find consumption booms (or either declines or stagnation of saving rates) in household sectors in both East Asia and Latin America in the early 1990s (Kohsaka, 1998). In fact, in East Asia, increases in public saving due to budget surplus and in corporate saving due to profit growth raised national saving rates. In other words, both regions had in common the fact that household consumption booms contributed to external imbalances in the period.

Anyway, once some macroeconomic imbalance in one country triggered a shift of market expectations and a resulting reversal of capital flow, it enforced self-fulfilling adjustments not only in that country but it also led to a sort of *country runs* via a contagious process in a region as a whole. Moreover, the more interdependent the economies within the region, the stronger this process worked through expected regional externalities. Thus, the real difference as far as the Asian currency crisis is concerned is that *both the degree and the scope of contagious results are disproportionately larger than the incipient imbalances of fundamentals*. Apparently, vulnerabilities of financial markets and corporate governance inherent to emerging markets as well as their increasing integration to the global market helps magnify a downward spiral of a self-fulfilling process of market expectations. Whether miracle or myth, East Asia has grown so large that the impact of their crisis on the growth scenario of the global economy cannot be negligible.

Table 5.2 Asian currency crisis and macroeconomic fundamentals, 1994–96 (%)

Country	*Current ac./GDP*	*GDP growth*	inflation	*Budget balance/GDP*	*S-T/ Total Debt*	*Debt service/ exports*	*Debt service/ GDP*
Indonesia	−2.1	7.8	8.6	1.4	21.3	32.8	8.9
Korean Republic	−2.5	8.2	5.2	0.2			
Malaysia	−6.6	9.0	4.2	3.0	23.4	8.1	8.3
Philippines	−4.3	5.0	8.5	0.6	15.7	16.2	6.9
Singapore	16.5	8.8	2.1	15.1			
Thailand	−7.2	8.1	5.6	2.3	45.1	12.2	5.2
Argentina	−1.9	2.4	2.6	−0.6	11.5	36.4	3.6
Brazil	−2.0	3.9	706.5		19.9	36.3	3.2
Chile	−1.7	6.6	9.0	2.1	26.2	25.8	7.5
Mexico	−2.7	1.3	25.4	−0.3	23.2	30.4	9.3
China	0.8	11.2	16.5	−1.8	18.7	9.2	2.1
Japan	2.1	1.9	0.2				
US	−1.9	2.8	2.8	−2.3			

Source: World Bank (1998) *World Development Indicators*.

IV DOMESTIC MACROECONOMIC MANAGEMENT: HOW TO COPE WITH THE INTERNATIONAL CAPITAL MARKET?

Macroeconomic imbalances by themselves would not trigger a currency crisis, but reversals of international capital flows based on depreciation expectations would. In this sense, macroeconomic imbalances are not a sufficient condition for a currency crisis. In the absence of macroeconomic imbalances, however, there would be no room for depreciation expectations to become overwhelming.[6] This might be the case for Singapore and Taiwan this time. Yet, we should note that reversals and/or reductions of capital flows would amplify necessary macroeconomic adjustments. Volatile capital flows are not only self-fulfilling but also destabilising. Keeping these in mind, let us consider policy implications to be drawn from the Asian currency crisis. We will discuss three separate aspects as follows: domestic macroeconomic management in this section, IMF prescriptions for crisis management in section V, and policy strategies against regional as well as global systemic risks in section VI.

What can we learn for macroeconomic management from a small open economy in the integrated global capital market? The virtual dollar-peg in Thailand was a challenge to the basic trilemma in macroeconomic policy where independent monetary policy, free capital mobility and exchange rate stability are mutually inconsistent. In order to maintain monetary autonomy, Thailand must either control capital flows or allow exchange rate flexibility (or balance them in between).

Next, should they have adopted free float? Probably, the answer is no. Thailand and other East Asian economies are small and open. Their degrees of openness (shares of external sector in domestic production/ expenditure) are as large as 30–90 per cent, and they take (not make) traded goods prices as given. Accordingly, exchange rate stability, which is almost equal to price stability, can be one of macroeconomic policy targets. Exchange rate stability, however, does not necessarily mean the dollar peg. Rather, the dollar peg induces excessive risk-taking by reducing exchange rate risks in US dollar-denominated transactions. The failure of exchange rate policies in Thailand existed not in exchange rate levels but in their inflexibility. We cannot avoid exchange rate risks, as long as major currencies float against each other. The dollar peg, where the monetary authorities take these risks, distorts expectation formation by the private sector, leading to excessive short-term borrowing from off-shore.

In East Asia, most economies have made allowances for exchange rate flexibility to some limited degree, monitoring overall stability of both nominal and real rates, though they appear to put an unproportionately larger weight on the US dollar than other major currencies. Indonesia, Korea, Malaysia and the Philippines are among them. Why then did they also suffer from currency attacks?

One may look at currency overvaluation for a possible reason. If exchange rate levels are too high with limited flexibility, external sectors would lose competitiveness and the resulting external imbalances must be corrected sooner or later. Now, if we look at real effective exchange rates in East Asia, there have been no explicit upward trends in Indonesia, Korea, Malaysia, Thailand and Taiwan since the late 1980s, while Hong Kong, the Philippines and Singapore show appreciation trends. Considering time lags in external adjustments by real rates,[7] therefore, deterioration in external balances in the former economies seems to be not because of exchange rate overvaluation but because of demand side or income effects.[8]

Thus, since flexible exchange rate management may not be sufficient to cope with currency speculation, we need to combine it with appropriate management of external borrowing (particularly of a short-term nature).[9] The present currency crisis exposed the difficulty small open emerging markets would have in attaining macroeconomic stability with exchange rate stability in the integrated international capital market. The access to the global market provides ample opportunities on the one hand but on the other, increases accompanying risks. Part of the latter consists of systemic risks inherent to the international capital market, which is beyond the scope of national governments' discretion.

V PITFALLS OF CRISIS MANAGEMENT: DEFLATIONARY POLICIES AND LIBERALISATION STRATEGY

The policy implications we can draw from the Asian currency crisis are not only limited to domestic policy authorities. The crisis also sent messages to such advisory institutions as the IMF, which imposes policy programmes as preconditions for its financial assistance. Among others, there seems to be some room for reconsideration of IMF prescriptions and their policy framework. One is on stabilisation policies and the other is on structural reforms.

Typical crises in developing economies in the past were mostly attributed to apparent internal and external macroeconomic imbalances, to which deflationary policies such as tightening of money and credit, restructuring of fiscal budgets, exchange rate devaluation and import controls have been applied. In the present crisis, however, even in severely affected economies, fiscal balances had been in surplus, domestic inflation mild, saving rates high and no cumulative overvaluation of currencies had been recorded. Yet, since those economies have been experiencing booms for years, domestic credit expansion raised asset prices, and then resulting investment exceeded saving more or less, thereby generating current account deficits. Accordingly, once asset prices started to fall and domestic currency values collapsed, balance sheets of corporate firms, as well as financial institutions, began to deteriorate, and then the latter began to squeeze credits. Thus, a deflationary spiral started to unwind.

Moreover, an additional negative factor must be noted at work in East Asia. That is, they have been highly leveraged economies. Their high growth had been supported mainly by financial intermediation instead of through capital markets. If we look at indicators of financial deepening, i.e. ratios of broad money to GDP (see Table 5.3), it is easy to see that they were significantly higher than in Latin America. Since this high-leveraged nature in itself is and had been a blessing rather than a handicap in terms of resource transfers in economic development, disruptions of this transfer mechanism, or the financial system, would magnify the deflationary impact referred to above.[10]

Table 5.3 Financial development, 1980–95 (M2/GDP, %)

Country	*1980*	*1985*	*1990*	*1995*
Indonesia	13.2	21.2	33.9	43.1
Korean Republic	35.8	39.8	54.3	79.4
Malaysia	46.1	61.2	63.1	85.0
Philippines	22.0	26.7	30.9	45.5
Singapore	57.7	71.0	83.5	80.9
Thailand	34.5	53.5	62.4	73.2
Argentina	19.0	10.3	6.2	18.8
Brazil	9.6	8.4	13.1	26.1
Chile	21.0	33.6	36.1	33.9
Mexico	25.2	21.5	17.5	26.8
China	33.2	47.3	70.3	92.4
Japan	83.4	91.9	110.8	112.1

Note: M3 GDP for Korea.
Sources: IMF (1998), IFS (1997) and World Bank, *World Development Indicators* (1998).

The crucial point here is that, in this situation, with the possibility of asset deflation, those classical deflationary policies mentioned above tend to aggravate a credit squeeze and are very likely to overkill aggregate demand. In contrast to typical crisis cases in developing economies, maintaining a certain positive level of output growth would have a crucial importance. Higher interest rates in the midst of currency crises would be of no use in preventing further depreciation, but would surely kill domestic consumption and investment. Deflationary monetary and fiscal measures would aggravate (rather than prevent from) the deflationary spiral and disrupt (rather than regain) confidence in the financial system. Even though we need to get rid of non-performed assets and non-performed financial institutions on the one hand, we have to maintain certain levels of domestic credit supply and give fiscal supports instead of reducing them, on the other, in order not to plunge into a pitfall of deflationary spirals.

Another problem of IMF prescription is that it hastily demands market-oriented reforms with deregulation and liberalisation in order to minimise inefficiencies due to government interventions. In fact, experiences of structural reforms since the 1980s have demonstrated that successful market liberalisation requires as a precondition adequate market infrastructure, while the latter can be established only over time. In this respect, Thailand gave us a good example. Over-borrowing from off-shore markets resulted from rapid domestic financial liberalisation and capital account deregulation without adequate monitoring and supervision by the monetary authorities in the 1990s. The crisis in Thailand taught us that, since adjustment speeds are generally large in financial markets, it is necessary to avoid hasty liberalisation and to strengthen a supervisory role of the authorities either prior to or along with liberalisation measures. Nevertheless, the IMF demands a strict implementation of structural (microeconomic) reforms as a conditional in its rescue programme, and this was the case this time.

Doubts on the effectiveness of IMF prescription seem to be shared by part of the market, because its rescue programme failed to stop further currency depreciation even after its conclusion. Though IMF claims that only monetary tightening can recover monetary discipline, short-term deflationary policies without doubt depress growth expectations. Long-term structural reforms as a conditionality would depress expectations further down. Since by definition structural reforms require difficult institutional changes, a rescue programme accompanying structural reforms as a conditionality would raise doubts on its feasibility and may generate expectations that an adjustment process would take longer time.

In the present international monetary regime, IMF loans have become a central factor even in the case of multilaterally coordinated rescue programmes. Accordingly, just as policy authorities' behaviour becomes endogenous in the economic system as a whole through private sector's expectations, IMF's behaviour has become endogenous through market expectations. Doubts on the effectiveness of IMF programmes and its smooth implementation affect the expectations on the duration of adjustments needed to get out of a crisis. We must note that, in the face of increasing capital market integration, the effect of market assessments of IMF programmes on adjustment processes has become far larger than before.

VI STRUCTURAL REFORM OF THE INTERNATIONAL MONETARY SYSTEM

At the end of Section IV, we mentioned the existence of systemic risks in the international capital market, which is beyond control of national governments. In this section we will discuss why the role of the IMF in alleviating this systemic risk is limited. One reason is in the nature of the international capital market, and the other is in the ability of IMF.

In the international capital market, emerging markets such as Thailand are marginal investment opportunities, and international investors regard them as more or less homogeneous. Put it in another way, information on those markets is incomplete, so that the investors do not know individual markets very well. When one prime minister in south-east Asia rebuked international investors for the Asian crisis and then his country's currency depreciated, it was said, 'the market assessed the policy (government)'. As we have seen, however, the market's ability in assessing policies is limited, too. Otherwise, it is incomprehensible why country ratings change abruptly overnight (Table 5.4).

A basic idea of an early warning system and obligatory reporting system of macroeconomic variables of individual national economies is that the more information available, the more likely the market discipline works. Yet, incomplete information in capital markets is not limited to developing economies, but inherent even to developed economies. Moreover, investors are well known to swing between exuberance and pessimism driven by a herd instinct. Good or bad, this is the way the market goes. While it is an improvement to enhance

Table 5.4 Market credit ratings: long-term foreign currency debt ratings, 1996–97

	15 Jan. 1996	*2 Dec. 1996*	*24 June 1997*	*12 Dec. 1997*
Moody's				
Indonesia	Baa3	Baa3	Baa3	Baa3
Malaysia	A1	A1	A1	A1
Philippines	Ba2	Ba2	Ba1	Ba1
Korea	A1	A1		Baa2
Thailand	A2	A2	A2	Baa1
Mexico	Ba2	Ba2	Ba2	Ba2
Standard & Poor's				
Indonesia	BBB	BBB	BBB	BBB–
Malaysia	A+	A+	A+	A+
Philippines	BB	BB	BB+	BB+
Korea	AA–	AA–		
Thailand	A	A	A	BBB
Mexico	BB	BB	BB	

Source: Radelet and Sachs (1998).

information availability, it could never completely eliminate inherent instability of market expectations.

How to cope with this systemic risk is a new policy issue revealed by the Asian currency crisis. The point is that, being aware of the above market failures, we are required to build a new global safety net against exchange rate instability in the face of ongoing trends of capital market integration. The present regime of rescue programmes with IMF as a core is revealing its limit in the present crisis.

Table 5.5 shows total amounts of rescue programmes and IMF loans within them in the Asian currency crisis. In the Mexican crisis, the total commitment amounted to US$50 billion. Turning to the Asian crisis, they amounted to US$17 billion for Thailand in August 1997, US$37 billion for Indonesia in October 1997 and US$58 billion for Korea in December 1997, among which IMF facilities were extended to from five to twenty times their original quotas. It is apparent that both sizes of rescue programmes and burdens of IMF have increased over time and along with deepening perception of seriousness of the crisis. IMF is to cover not only Asia and Latin America but also Middle East, Africa and transition economies. As such, considering further growth of emerging market economies and their integration to the international capital market in the long run, the present rescue

Table 5.5 Commitments to Asian crisis countries[a]

Country	*IMF*	*(% of quota)*	*Year*	*Multilateral*	*Bilateral*	*Total*
Thailand	3.9	(505)	8/97	2.7	10.5	17.1
Indonesia	9.9	(490)	11/97	8.0	18.7	36.6
Korea	20.9	(1939)	12/97	14.0	23.3	58.2
Total	34.7			24.7	52.5	111.9

Note: [a] In US$ bn.
Source: IMF [1998a].

regime has apparently reached its limit, and will be unable to cope with a next wave of contagious currency crises.

VII CONCLUDING REMARKS

As the Asian currency crisis is new as far as the aspects mentioned above, policy strategies taken so far may have to be understood as a trial-and-error attempt. Indeed, the IMF not only modified original programmes in order to make its intermediate goal budgetary flexibility, mitigating monetary tightness and strengthening the social safety net but also was said to have begun efforts to strengthen the architecture of the international financial system (IMF, 1998a). But, the social costs due to the lost confidence in the financial system may be too huge to recover, and we are committed not to just modify, but to restructure our policy strategies against the present as well as future crises.

One of the basic lessons we have to learn from the present crisis would be the perception of both inherent vulnerability of emerging markets and the volatility of the international capital market. Of course, it is important to strengthen capital markets and straighten corporate governance in emerging markets as well as in developed economies in the long run, but policy strategies should have taken the vulnerability as given in the short and/or medium run. Also, it is essential to reform structures of individual emerging as well as developed economies in order to adapt to the developing economic environment, but it may be equally essential to reform the international safety net including multilateral institutions.

Possible regional financial cooperation may give one example in this direction. As pointed out earlier, one particular aspect of this recent

Asian currency crisis is that regional externalities worked negatively in market expectations. In order to cope with them, it may be useful to build a regional cooperative framework as a safety net against regional crisis contagion like the *Tom-Yam* effect. The idea of an Asian Monetary Fund was born immediately after the crisis had gone, because it was thought that the Fund may have been redundant as far as financing and consulting facilities were concerned in the presence of the IMF, and that, emphasising the role of immediate liquidity supply to problem economies, it may have aggravated moral hazard there.

As the appropriate architecture for the global safety net would not be in place straightaway, an idea of a regional currency stabilisation fund with functions of consultation on macroeconomic policies, of peer monitoring over currency and capital markets and of mutual foreign exchange financing within the region would be worthwhile considering, because exchange rate stability is one of the essential factors that has supported and will support growth performances of the closely knitted regional economies in East Asia.

Notes

1. This paper was presented at the 6th Biannual Convention of EAEA, Kitakyushu, Japan, 4–5 September 1998.
2. For structural changes in foreign capital flows and their mechanism in the Asia Pacific region, see, for example, Kohsaka (1996).
3. For example, the IMF admitted that its staff did not forecast the recent crises and was too optimistic in its projection, though they gave warnings about the dangers associated with financial sector weaknesses (IMF, 1997).
4. In Thailand, a series of financial deregulation measures were adopted in the early 1990s, which included deregulation of control of commercial banks' foreign exchange positions and outward capital transactions, and establishment of off-shore financial market (Bangkok International Banking Facility), and its related incentive measures.
5. Some empirical studies identify that the main trigger of the Mexican crisis was the reversal of international interest rates rather than domestic macroeconomic imbalances. See, for example, Fernandez-Arias (1996).
6. Political instability could be a trigger for a currency crisis. In Hong Kong in 1983, the conflict between China and the UK over the return of the island caused Hong Kong dollar depreciation under the free float regime. In Mexico in 1994, a series of currency attacks were aroused by such political uncertainty factors as an assassination, a political scandal, and a guerilla eruption. In both cases, however, there existed macroeconomic imbalances prior to the crises.

7. For example, IMF (1995) found that, while changes in real activity affect trade flow immediately, the effect of changes in real exchange rate rises only over time.
8. Many economists argue that overvaluation of currencies were part of reasons for external imbalances in the Asian currency crisis (for example, Stiglitz, 1998). Indeed, if we look at movements of real effective exchange rates from the peak of high-yen/low-dollar in April 1995, their rises in East Asia were far from insignificant, in the high end, for example, 15 per cent increase in two years in Thailand. But, if you observe their medium-run trends in the 1990s, their real effective exchange rates were not persistently high. So that, we would not be able to attribute the revealed real appreciation in 1996 to deterioration in their external balances in the same year.
9. In fact, even IMF has recently become more generous on short-term capital controls (IMF, 1997).
10. For example, it is argued that Mexico suffered relatively little from asset deflation (IMF, 1997). Kregel [1999] asserts that the Asian crisis was debt deflation as against the Mexican balance of payments crisis.

References

(BIS) 1993 Bank for International Settlements 1997, *Annual Report 1996/97.*

Bhanupong Nidhiprabha (1997) 'Macroeconomic management and development process: the southeast Asian perspective', a paper presented at the Workshop on Comparative African & East Asian Development Experiences, Johannesburg, South Africa, 3–6 Nov. 1997.

Caprio, Gerard Jr and Daniela Klingebiel (1997) 'Bank insolvency: bad luck, bad policy, or bad banking?' in *Annual World Bank Conference on Development Economics 1996.*

Eichengreen, Barry, Andrew K. Rose and Charles Wyplosz (1996) 'Contagious currency crisis', NBER Working Paper No. 5681, July.

Feldstein, Martin (1998) 'Refocusing the IMF', *Foreign Affairs*, Mar./ Apr.

Fernandez-Arias, Eduardo (1996) 'The new wave of private capital inflows: push or pull?' *Journal of Development Economics*, vol. 48, pp. 389–418.

Glick, Reuven and Ramon Moreno (1994) 'Capital flows and monetary policy in east asia', *Pacific Basin Working Paper Series*, No. PB94–08, Federal Reserve Bank of San Francisco, 1994.

IMF (International Monetary Fund) (1995) 'Exchange rate movements and their impacts on trade and investment in the APEC region', *IMF Discussion Paper*, Oct. 1995.

IMF (1997) *World Economic Outlook: Interim Assessment*, Dec.

IMF (1998a) *The IMF's Response to the Asian Crisis*, IMF Homepage, 15 June.

IMF (1998b) *World Economic Outlook*, May.

Kohsaka, Akira (1996) 'Interdependence through capital flows in the Pacific Asia and the role of Japan' in T. Ito and A.O. Krueger (eds), *Financial Deregulation and Integration in East Asia* (Chicago: University of Chicago Press).

Kohsaka, Akira (ed.) (1998) *Domestic Saving in the Pacific Region*, Pacific Economic Outlook/Structure, Japan Committee for Pacific Economic Outlook, Kansai Economic Research Center, 1998.

Kregel, J.A. (1999) 'East Asia is not Mexico: the Difference between Balance of Payments Crises and Debt Deflation', in Jomo K S (ed.), *Tigers in Trouble: Financial Governance, Liberalization and Crises in East Asia* (London : Zed Press).

Milesi-Ferretti, Gian Maria (1996) 'Sustainability of persistent current account deficits', *NBER Working Paper* No. 5467, Feb.

Obstfeld, Maurice and Alan M. Taylor (1997) 'The Great Depression as a watershed: international capital mobility over the long run', *NBER Working Paper* No. 5960, Mar.

Radelet, Steven and Jeffrey Sachs (1998) 'The onset of the East Asian financial crisis', mimeograph, Feb.

Sachs, Jeffrey D. (1997) 'IMF is a power unto itself', *The Financial Times*, 11 Dec.

Sachs, Jeffrey D., Aaron Turnell and Andres Velasco (1996) 'Financial crises in emerging markets: the lessons from 1995', *Brookings Papers on Economic Activity*, vol. 1.

Stiglitz, Joseph (1998) 'The role of international financial institutions in the current global economy', Address to the Chicago Council on Foreign Relations, World Bank Homepage, 27 Feb.

World Bank (1997) *International Financial Statistics*.

World Bank (1998) *World Development Indicators*.

6 Liberalisation, the stock market and the market for corporate control: a bridge too far for the Indian economy?*

Ajit Singh

INTRODUCTION

An outstanding development of the 1990s, closely associated with the economic reform programme initiated by Dr Manmohan Singh, has been the very fast expansion of the stockmarkets and their growing role in the Indian economy. Both internal and external liberalisation measures, undertaken as a part of the financial reform, as well as the more liberal general economic ethos created by the reform, have largely been responsible for this evolution.

The first part of this chapter reviews the stock market reforms and comments on the available evidence on the effects of stock market expansion on corporate growth and on the real economy. The second part focuses on the proposed next stage of the reform, being urged by the financial community. Their specific proposal is to establish a market for corporate control in order to maximise the benefits from stock market development. The government has recently published a Takeover Code which suggests that it is not opposed to the evolution of such a market.

Takeovers and a corporate control market would have far-reaching effects on the Indian economy, but there has been little informed debate on this subject. This chapter attempts to invite such a debate by putting forward analyses and evidence to suggest that this reform is

---

* The author, editors and publishers are grateful to Oxford University Press, New Delhi, for permission to reproduce this chapter from *India's Economic Reform and Development*, edited by Ahluwalia and Little (1998).

more likely to harm than help the real economy at India's present stage of development. The proposed reform should therefore be resisted.

ECONOMIC REFORM AND STOCKMARKET DEVELOPMENT[1]

Although India has long had a stock market, its development after independence and up until 1980 ebbed and flowed but in general had been quite slow. In 1980, the total market capitalisation on the Indian stockmarkets as a proportion of GDP was only 5 per cent. By 1990, following the liberalisation measures initiated during the 1980s, the ratio rose to 13 per cent. With the accelerated pace of liberalisation under Dr Singh's reforms the stock market growth has been explosive. By end-1993, total market capitalisation reached 60 per cent of GDP.

Between 1980 and 1993, the number of mutual funds investors rose from 2 to 40 million, a figure second only to the US (51 million). In terms of listed companies, the Indian stock market (7,985 companies in 1995) is now the largest in the world, larger even than the US (7,671 companies), with the UK (2,078 companies) and Germany (678 companies) far behind.[2]

The daily turnover of shares on the Bombay stock exchange rose from 0.13 billion Rupees in 1980–81 to 3.7 billion Rupees in 1993–94, an almost thirty-fold increase. The average daily trading volume on the Bombay market in the early 1990s was similar to that in London – about 45,000 trades a day. At its peak trading has occurred at double that rate.

Although Indian stockmarket growth during the 1980s and 1990s has been impressive, so has it been in several other leading emerging markets. In Taiwan market capitalisation as a proportion of GDP rose from 11 per cent in 1981 to 74 per cent in 1991. Similarly, between 1983 and 1993, the Chilean ratio rose from 13.2 per cent to 78 per cent and the Thai from 3.8 per cent to 55.8 per cent. To put these figures in an historical perspective, Mullins (1993) notes that it probably took the US stockmarket 85 years (1810–95) to achieve a broadly similar increase in capitalisation ratio, from 7 per cent to 71 per cent.

In Indian stockmarket reforms, liberalisation has occurred simultaneously with fresh regulation (Joshi and Little 1996). Liberalisation measures have included the repeal of the Capital Issues Control Act 1947 by which the government controlled new share issues and determined the issue price. Externally, liberalisation has allowed foreign institutional investors to directly purchase Indian corporate shares. Similarly, Indian companies have been permitted to raise funds abroad.[3]

The flagship of the goverment's new regulations to ensure transparency and above board functioning of stockmarkets has been the Securities and Exchange Board of India Act which came into force in January 1992. Under this act, the authorities have attempted to regulate the activities of stock brokers, merchant banks and other intermediaries on the primary market. Although the Securities and Exchange Board of India (SEBI) has apparently made progress in some areas, it will be a long time before the Indian stockmarket loses its justly deserved reputation as being a 'snake pit' to use Joshi and Little's expressive phrase. Mayya (1995) notes the continuing huge malpractices on the secondary markets.[4]

THE STOCKMARKET, CORPORATE GROWTH AND THE REAL ECONOMY

How has this enormous stock market expansion affected the real economy? Has it brought about larger savings and investment or greater productivity of investment as the stock market proponents suggest?[5]

The financing of corporate growth

At first sight, the answer appears highly positive. During the 1980s and the 1990s, the Indian corporations have raised large amounts of capital on a very active primary market to finance their growth. In 1980, 929 million rupees were raised through corporate securities issuance (Balasubramanian, 1993). This figure had risen to 2.5 billion rupees by 1985, to a huge 123 billion rupees by 1990, and by 1993–94, it reached 225 billion rupees, i.e. a 250-fold increase since 1980. By contrast, general price levels rose less than four-fold during this period. New corporate securities constituted 12.8 per cent of the country's gross domestic savings in 1993–94 (Mayya, 1995). Another indicator of an extremely active primary market is that in 1994–95 nearly 1,700 companies raised equity capital (either through direct offerings to the public or through rights issues); of these, 369 were new companies (RBI, 1995).

Singh (1995b) has examined the financing of corporate growth in 10 industrialising economies (including India) during the 1980s at a micro-economic level. His sample for each country normally consisted of the 100 largest listed manufacturing companies which existed throughout the period 1980–90. Table 6.1, reporting his results for India, indicates that the average Indian corporation, during the 1980s, financed about 40 per cent of its growth of 'net assets' (the long-term capital employed in the firm) from internal sources (i.e. retained profits) and 60 per cent from external sources. Of the latter, nearly a third came from equity issues and two-thirds from long-term debt. The three financing variables obey the basic accounting identity that the total growth of net assets equals the sum of the internal and external sources of finance. The above results pertain to 1980–90, but in view of the enormous stock market activity in the 1990s, the importance of stock market finance, would be even greater for the later period.

This large recourse to external and particularly stock market finance by the Indian companies is theoretically surprising as is the great number of stock market listings. An underdeveloped capital market, by its inability to provide the desired external finance, may be expected to oblige corporations to grow largely from internal sources. Moreover, in an imperfect stock market, which operates like a 'snake pit', firms would be discouraged from raising stock market finance and indeed from seeking a listing at all. Economic theory suggests that in an emerging stock market, where information gathering and dissemination activity is not adequately developed, and where most firms have not yet built a 'reputation', the pricing of the firms' shares will tend to be arbitrary and volatile (Tirole, 1991). This should discourage risk-averse firms from raising stock market finance. Moreover, developing country firms are likely to be family-controlled, which should also inhibit them from issuing new equity for the fear of losing control.

Further, as Schleifer and Vishny (1996) note, if there is inadequate legal protection for the investments of minority shareholders (as is common in emerging markets), one would expect households, or even prudent institutions, not to buy company shares.

It will be useful in this context to consider the financing of corporate growth in advanced countries. These corporations are widely thought to follow a 'pecking order' according to which firms rely largely, if not entirely, on internal sources to finance their growth. If more finance is needed, they use long-term loans or bank borrowings, and only as a very last resort go to the stock market to raise funds. When there is a separation of ownership and control, and when managers are able to pursue their own goals, it is not difficult to see why firms may shun the stockmarket. For management-controlled corporations, internal finance is clearly a cheaper and easier source of finance than the stock market where financing is only available subject to wide public

Table 6.1 India: Top 100 listed companies in manufacturing, 1980–90 quartile distributions of indicators of financing of corporate growth: after tax retention ratio, internal and external financing of growth[1] (%)

	Retention ratio (A.T) (long-term)	*Internal finance (long-term)*	*External finance equity (long-term)*	*External finance (long-term development funds) (long-term)*
Lower quartile (Q1)	55.0	23.9	3.6	24.2
Median (Q2)	68.0	38.1	16.3	38.9
Upper quartile (Q3)	76.2	62.0	31.5	57.8
Mean	65.7	40.5	19.6	39.9
Std dev.	15.0	32.8	21.9	24.4
Skewness	–0.60	–0.80	0.67	0.29
Kurtosis	0.59	3.10	0.57	–0.01

Note: [1] Averaged over the whole period, normally from 1980 to 1990.
Source: Singh (1997b).

Table 6.2 All countries: top listed companies in manufacturing: financing of corporate growth: after tax retention ration,[1] internal and external finance of growth:[1] median values

Country	*No. of companies*	*Period*	*Retention ratio (AT) (%)*	*Internal finance (%)*	*External finance equity (%)*	*External finance ltd. (%)*
Korea	100	1980–90	65.7	15.8	46.9	30.4
Pakistan	100	1980–88	65.9	67.5	5.2	23.9
Jordan	38	1980–90	48.0	54.8	25.5	5.8
Thailand	67	1983–90	48.7	14.7	n.a.	n.a.
Mexico	100	1084–90	n.a.	23.1	64.7	1.0
India	100	1980–90	68.0	38.1	16.3	38.9
Turkey	45	1982–90	37.8	13.4	66.6	16.9
Malaysia	100	1983–90	51.7	29.7	48.0	12.0
Zimbabwe	48	1980–88	61.7	57.0	43.5	0.0
Brazil	100	1985–91	98.3	46.0	37.2	5.6
All			62.9	32.0	41.13	16.0
P^2 [1]			155.6[2]	147.45[2]	185.3[2]	121.4[2]

Notes:
[1] Average values for the relevant period for each country. P^2 statistic for comparison of medians across countries.
[2] implies rejection of the null hypothesis of equality of medians.
Source: Singh (1995b).

scrutiny. However, in a classic contribution, Myers and Majluf (1984) showed that if there was asymmetric information between managers and shareholders, it would be rational even for profit-maximising managers to follow the above 'pecking order'.

Myers and Majluf's general argument applies equally to developing country corporations. However, although the average Indian firm in Table 6.1 does deviate somewhat from the expected 'pecking order', it is its heavy reliance on external finance and the considerable use of equity finance which are theoretically more anomalous for the reasons outlined earlier. However, Table 6.2, which provides comparative data for ten industrialising countries, shows that the Indian case is by no means unique. The typical Korean corporation financed more than 80 per cent of its growth of net assets from external sources. The corresponding figures for Turkey, Mexico and Thailand are 84.7 per cent, 75.6 per cent and 72.3 per cent respectively. Table 6.2 also shows that corporations in several sample countries resorted to equity finance during the 1980s to an even greater degree than their counterparts in India. The 'pecking order' theory is comprehensively violated for nearly half the sample countries. Singh (1994, 1995b) has provided an explanation of these anomalous phenomena (including that of the large number of listings in markets such as India's) in terms of: (a) the special circumstances of developing country financial markets in the 1980s; (b) the situation in advanced country markets; and (c) and the encouragement of stockmarket growth by developing country governments in order, *inter alia*, to implement privatisation.

Is the contribution of equity finance to Indian corporate growth overstated?

In a recent paper, Cobham and Subhramaniam (1995) (C & S hereafter) suggest that the methodology used in Table 1 overstates the contribution of equity finance to Indian corporate growth and therefore exaggerates the apparently positive role of the stockmarket. Using the alternative methodology of Mayer (1990) and Corbett and Jenkinson (1994) (MCJ hereafter), the C & S estimate of the contribution of new equity to Indian corporate investment is considerably smaller.

The differences in the empirical results are indeed due to the different methodologies used in the two exercises. The respective methods, however, have important implications for economic interpretation of the results. The following points are salient.

First, MCJ include depreciation as a major component of internal finance, whereas in Singh (1995b), as in Tables 6.1 and 6.2, it is excluded both from the numerator and the denominator in the relevant ratios. As Singh's research is concerned with measuring the sources of finance for corporate *growth* of 'net assets', it necessarily focuses on the *net* increase in corporate assets – the depreciation provision for replacement is normally require dto merely maintain the stock of assets (see futher Prais, 1976 for a classic discussion).

Secondly, the MCJ method, when used with the flow-of-funds data (as is generally the case), relates to the corporate sector as a whole, rather than to the individual firms. In this approach intra-corporate sector transactions are normally 'netted out' and external finance means funds from outside the corporate sector. Therefore, the question being addressed by MCJ with the flow-of-funds data is: how is 'investment' of the corporate sector as a whole financed, by internal sources (with the corporate sector) and by external sources (from outside the sector, e.g. the household or the financial sector). This is a different question from that addressed by Singh, who uses firm-level accounting data to enquire how individual corporations, rather than the corporate sector as a whole, finance the growth of their net assets, net of depreciation.

Thirdly, the differences in the corporate financing patterns between developed and developing countries are greatly reduced when these patterns are estimated by the use of the same methodology – whether MCJ or Singh (see further Singh, 1995b).

In short, the MCJ and the Singh methods are addressing different questions: the latter is concerned with the growth of corporate 'net' rather than 'gross assets', and is considering the financing question from the perspective of the individual firm rather than that of the corporate sector as a whole.

However, leaving aside these methodological issues, two things are clear: (1) the stock market has made a far greater contribution in the 1980s and the 1990s to Indian corporate growth than it ever did before, and (2) the observed pattern of corporate financing for India and several other industrialising countries runs contrary to theoretical expectations.

The stock market financing of corporate growth and the real economy

An important reason why so much finance was raised from the stock market by the Indian corporate sector in the 1980s and 1990s was the share price boom which occurred during this period. The Bombay Sensitive Index rose from 123.6 in 1980 to 396.4 in 1985, to 1,040.7 in

1990 to 2,222 in 1992, to over 4,000 by the summer of 1994. However, the market has slumped over the following two years, as is reflected in the end-year index values: 1994, 3,845; 1995, 3,109; and 1996, 3,104.

Confining attention for analytical purposes to the decade 1980–90, there was a well over eight-fold increase in share prices, while consumer prices rose by less than 10 per cent per annum during this period. Singh (1995b) estimated that between 1980 and 1985, the total (dividend plus capital gains) nominal return to a stock market investment was 33 per cent and the real return was 23 per cent; the corresponding nominal and real returns for the period 1986 to 1990 were 26 per cent and 18 per cent respectively, which gives an average real return of 20 per cent for the decade as a whole.

There is agreeement that the stock market boom of the 1980s was largely policy-induced (Balasubramanian, 1993; Nagaraj, 1996). By the early 1980s, neither the development finance institutions (DFIs) nor the commercial banks could meet their government-imposed requirements to lend to the priority sectors at concessional rates and also meet the private corporate needs. The Reserve Bank of India therefore advised the mobilisation of household savings through capital market expansion for meeting the corporate sector's requirements. This led to several fiscal incentives which helped to increase greatly the number of investors on the stock market, mainly through the growth of mutual funds. In that sense the post-1991 reforms can be regarded as a continuation of the process which began in the 1980s.

The stock market boom created by the entry of large number of domestic and subsequently foreign investors (as external liberalisation proceeded in the 1990s) into the capital market, lowered the cost of capital for the Indian corporations enacouraging them to raise large amounts of stock market finance. A central question is: has this benefited the real economy?

There is scant empirical work on this subject, but an important recent contribution by Nagaraj (1996) provides very useful information for the period 1980–91. His relevant findings are as follows:

1. The huge increase in stock market financing activity is not associated with either a rise in aggregrate gross domestic savings, or equally significantly, with an increase in the proportion of financial savings. Gross domestic savings as a proportion of GDP at market prices reached its peak level of 23 per cent in 1978–79. The savings ratio was, however, generally lower throughout the 1980s, and not higher. The financial proportion of the gross domestic

savings fell from its peak level of 55 per cent in 1984–85 to 42–45 per cent in the second half of the decade. However, there was a big change in the composition of financial savings. The share of corporate debentures and equities in total financial savings rose from 3.3 per cent in the 1970s to 6 per cent in the first half of the 1980s, and to 11.8 per cent in the second half of the decade. Over the same periods, the corresponding figures for bank deposits were 45 per cent, 39 per cent and 27 per cent respectively. Thus, the enormous stock market activity in the 1980s basically involved a portfolio substitution by households and institutions from bank deposits towards stock market instruments.

2. Using both aggregate accounting as well as the flow-of-funds data for the private corporate sector as a whole, Nagaraj reports a considerable fall in the 1980s in the proportion of either gross or net fixed capital formation which was financed through internal sources, i.e. retained earnings or depreciation. This combined with other evidence in his paper suggests that the increase in external finance available to the corporate sector through the capital market appears, to an appreciable extent, to have replaced corporations' internal funds during this decade. This could in part be due to a decline in corporate profitability (see below).
3. Importantly, Nagaraj also reports some increase in the corporate sector's gross fixed capital formation as a proportion of (a) GDP at market prices, and (b) of the aggregate fixed capital formation. However, whether this observed increase can be ascribed to the growth of the capital raised on the stock market is more problematical. Nagaraj finds that whereas there was previously a statistically positive correlation between the annual growth rates of capital raised externally and the corporate fixed capital formation, the relationship between the two variables (including that with suitable lags) has become statistically insignificant in the 1980s. It is, however, still positive but the value of the coefficient is much smaller (0.25 between 1980–81 to 1990–92, versus 0.45 between 1961–62 to 1979–80)
4. On the question of whether or not the stock market activity has led to improved productivity of investment, Nagaraj provides two pieces of evidence. First, he finds that the growth rate of real value added in the corporate manufacturing sector in the 1980s was lower than that of the registered manufacturing sector as a whole. This suggests that the smaller non-corporate firms which did not have access to stock market funds were able to grow at a faster

rate than the larger corporate firms. Secondly, there was a secular decline in corporate profitability during the 1980s, a result which is similar to that of Singh (1996b) for the 100 largest Indian quoted companies. Of course, it could be argued that the fall in profitability does not indicate a decline in efficiency, but that it simply reflects greater product market competition as a result of general liberalisation.

The above hypothesis can fortunately be tested on the data available in the IFC data bank which permits a decomposition of the rate of return into two components: the profit margin (profits/sales) and output–capital ratio (sales/net assets). The results show that the secular fall in the profitability of the 100 largest firms in the 1980s was entirely due to a decrease in the productivity of capital rather than a reduction in profit margins. The latter event is what would have been expected if the fall in profitability had been caused by greater product market competition.

Nevertheless, it could still be argued within a neoclassical framework that reduced profitability does not necessarily indicate inefficiency since the real cost of capital has fallen. The latter, however, was caused by the stock market boom which was by no means permanent. This leads to a related point which is concerned with the volatility of share prices. Share prices in India in recent years have been highly volatile (El-Erian and Kumar, 1995). Apart from the other drawbacks of volatility, we note in the present context that it reduces the efficiency of the stock market pricing signals for allocating investment resources (Tirole, 1991).

In assessing the effects of stock market expansion on the real economy, in addition to its effect on savings, investment and the productivity of investment, it is also necessary to examine the impact of foreign portfolio capital inflows. As a consequence of the government's external liberalisation measures in the post-1991 period, there was a huge increase in such flows. Joshi and Little (1996) report that non-debt creating private capital inflows in 1993/94 amounted to $4.1 billion and to $4.9 billion in 1994/95. Nearly three-quarters of these comprised portfolio equity capital, including share issues by Indian companies on overseas stock markets.

At one level, these capital inflows helped the real economy. The flows contributed to resolving the liquidity crisis of 1991 and to assisting the central bank to build up sizeable foreign exchange reserves; the latter reached a high point of nearly $20 billion in 1994/95.

Ironically, these foreign exchange reserves helped to reduce the government's dependence on the IMF giving it greater freedom to pursue a more independent economic policy or if it was politically required.

However, the government has also been keenly aware of the dangers of such inflows. Although these inflows were non-debt creating, the could not be regarded as being permanent. As Singh (1997a; 1997b) points out, a sudden withdrawal of these portfolio flows for totally extraneous reasons could lead to a negative interaction between two inherently unstable markets, the currency and the stock markets, which could do enormous damage to the real economy (as happened in Mexico). The Indian government has generally followed pragmatic policies and has used sterilisation and taxation measues to discourage short-term inflows. The present author would concur with Joshi and Little's (1996) judgement that the government policy in this area has been broadly sensible. Although portfolio capital inflows do create serious macroeconomic difficulties, the government policy measures have so far stopped them from doing any harm to the real economy.

To sum up, the available evidence suggests that despite the benefits of stock market expansion to the corporate sector, the real economy in the 1980s does not appear to have benefited from either increased savings and investment or a greater productivity of investment. On the other hand, the government's policy has prevented any harm to the real economy from the huge capital inflow surges of 1993/94 and 1994/95. It should, however, also be recorded that the evidence on savings, investments and investment productivity outlined above refers to the period 1980–90. The data for the 1990s could in principle lead to a more favourable verdict. Nevertheless, it is worth noting that the real economy, particularly industry has achieved its fastest growth in the last two years when the stock market has not been doing well. During 1995/96 and 1996/97 the real economy has expanded at a rate of nearly 7 per cent per annum – quite unprecedented for India. In the same period, the Bombay Sensitive Index has fallen from its peak of over 4,000 in the summer of 1994 to 3,104 on 31 December 1996. All this would suggest that the stock market may have so far been a 'sideshow' with relatively little impact, positive or negative, on the aggregate real economy. However, with the advent of the market for corporate control, the stock market will become much less of a sideshow. It is likely to come to play a much more prominent role in the real economy, arguably to the latter's considerable disadvantage as will be suggested below.

THE MARKET FOR CORPORATE CONTROL: THEORY AND EVIDENCE

Takeovers and the Stockmarket: Analytical Considerations

In textbook theory, takeovers provide an important additional mechanism through which the stock market can promote a more efficient utilisation of capital resources. There are two distinct ways in which the establishment of a market for corporate control may do this:

1. The *threat* of takeovers may lead inefficient firms to perform better.
2. Even if all firms were on their efficiency frontier the amalgamation of some through the *act* of takeovers may lead to a better social allocation of resources via synergy.

Moreover, there are many quoted companies which hardly ever raise stock market finance as they have adequate internal sources for their expansion. Such firms cannot therefore be disciplined by the normal pricing process of the stock market whereby the efficient companies are rewarded with, other things being equal, high share prices and a lower cost of capital and the inefficient firms face a higher cost of capital. However, even these firms, if they are inefficient, would be subject to the direct sanctions of the market for corporate control.

Nevertheless, more recent economic analysis suggests several reasons why these potential virtues of a market for corporate control may not actually materialise in the real world. To summarise:

1. Real world markets for corporate control even in advanced economies are subject to an inherent imperfection: it is far easier for a large firm to take over a small one than the other way around Singh (1971, 1975, 1992). Although a small efficient firm can in principle take over a large inefficient corporation (and to some degree this did happen in the US takeover wave of the 1980s through 'junk bonds'), its incidence is very small (Hughes, 1991).

   This consideration is particularly important for developing countries like India where there are large, potentially predatory conglomerate groups (Singh, 1995b). These could take over smaller, more efficient firms and thereby reduce potential competition to the detriment of the real economy. In a takeover battle it is the absolute firepower (absolute size) which counts rather than relative efficiency.

2. The efficient operation of takeover mechanism requires that enormous quantities of information are widely available – specifically, how profitable is each firm under its existing management and what would be its potential under any other management if it were taken over. Such information is not easily available even in advanced countries (Helm, 1989). For reasons discussed earlier, it would be far scarcer in emerging markets.
3. There are in practice huge transactions costs involved in takeovers in countries like the US and the UK which hinder the efficiency of the takeover mechanism. Changing management through takeover turns out to be a very expensive way of accomplishing this task (Peacock and Bannock, 1991). This consideration is particularly important for developing countries which can ill afford such high transactions costs.
4. Recent work based on asymmetric information, signalling and involving the concept of signal jamming suggests that the market for corporate control may not just be inefficient but may in fact generate perverse outcomes. Stein (1989) showed that under plausible assumptions if the information about the firm's operations is, or is perceived to be asymmetric, it may pay rational managers even in rational markets to be myopic. This would lead to short-termism and to lower rates of investment than would otherwise be the case – an issue which is particularly significant for developing countries trying to achieve fast economic growth.
5. A similar socially perverse outcome of the takeover process has been suggested by Schleifer and Summers (1988). They point out that the takeover mechanism in the US is often used as a device not to honour the implicit contracts of workers in the acquired firm with the pre-acquisition management. Such abandonment of implicit contracts according to the authors is socially harmful because it discourages firm-specific accumulation of human capital by workers.

   Takeovers could also in principle reduce previous over-manning. Which outcome actually prevails will depend on the specific circumstances. It may be suggested that in countries like India with strong employment protection laws, the Schleifer and Summers' line of reasoning is not relevant. However, if such laws were to be repealed under the economic reform, this argument will become significant.
6. Grossman and Hart (1980) have suggested that because of the 'free-rider' problem, the takeover mechanism may not work efficiently. Any individual shareholder may feel that their action is

> unlikely to affect the outcome of a disciplinary takeover bid. It would therefore be best not to accept a raider's offer and to wait until the share price increases further after the successful bid. Grossman and Hart argued that if all shareholders act in this way, the disciplinary takeover bids would not materialise. Indeed in these circumstances, raiders will not have adequate incentives to undertake such bids at all.

The Grossman and Hart theory, however, applies only to disciplinary bids. In practice, it is difficult to distinguish between such raids and those undertaken for other motives, for example, empire-building or increasing monopoly power. The latter motives, however, are likely to be very relevant in many emerging markets because of the presence in these countries, as mentioned earlier, of large conglomerate business groups.

Evidence on takeovers

Although there are embryonic markets for corporate control in a few developing countries (e.g. Brazil, and for that matter even in India[6]), most do not yet have hostile takeovers and fully fledged markets for control. The evidence on the characteristics and operations of such markets can therefore only come from advanced countries such as the UK and the US.

Selection process and the threat of takeovers

Singh (1971, 1975) were among the first studies to examine systematically the nature of the selection process in the market for corporate control. This involved a comparative analysis of the multivariate characteristics of four kinds of populations of firms: the acquired, the acquiring, the non-acquired, and the non-acquiring. Singh's research was based on takeovers in the UK and covered two periods – one of normal takeover activity (1954 to 1960); and the other of the takeover boom of 1967 to 1970. His results have proved to be extremely robust and have been confirmed in most subsequent studies both for the UK and the US.[7]

The central finding of the Singh's exercises can be summarised as follows. Contrary to the expectations of neoclassical theory as well as the folklore of capitalism, selection in the market for corporate control does not take place entirely on the basis of efficiency, i.e. profitability or stock market valuation. Although profitability matters, absolute size matters much more. A relatively unprofitable large company has a much better chance of survival than a small profitable company. Moreover, it is almost always the large which takeover the small. Thus the acquisition process may indeed act in a perverse way since a large unprofitable company can increase its immunity to takeovers through the takeover process itself – by becoming bigger through the acquisition of small firms.[8]

Effects of takeovers: microeconomic efficiency

Apart from the threat of takeovers and the nature of the selection process, there is a large literature for industrial countries on the effects of actual takeovers on the post-merger efficiency of acquiring firms. Here there is an important divide between industrial organisation studies based on accounting data and studies by financial specialists which use stock market data. The former invariably show that on average, controlling for the effects of industry and of the business cycle, the post-merger profitability of the amalgamating merging firms declines relative to their weighted average of the pre-merger profitability of the amalgamating merging firms declines relative to their weighted average of the pre-merger profitability. Since the amalgamated firm is likely to have greater (and certainly no less) monopoly power than the pre-merger firms considered on their own, this empirical finding is interpreted as indicating mergers lead on average to a decline in micro-economic efficiency.

A radically different view of the efficiency of mergers comes from specialists in finance who use stock market data and the so-called 'event studies' methodology to investigate the effects of mergers. Here the basic empirical finding is that in the period immediately preceding the takeover event there is on average an appreciation of the value of the victim firm by about 20 per cent, while the raider's stockmarket value either remains the same or appreciates or depreciates by a relatively small amount. Since the overall result of the merger is an increase of about 20 per cent on average in the stockmarket value of the amalgamating firms, finance specialists conclude that this reflects an increase in net social welfare.

This inference is, however, subject to an extremely important qualification. It is valid only if the real world share prices are always efficient in Tobin's (1984) fundamental valuation sense, i.e. relative share prices of firms reflecting their relative (rationally) expected earnings. There is considerable support for the hypothesis that share prices are, broadly speaking, efficient in what Tobin calls 'the information arbitrage' sense, i.e. that all information percolates quickly in the market and is therefore immediately reflected in the price. Such efficiency, however, does not necessarily imply efficiency in the fundamental valuation sense. There is a large body of analytical and empirical work to indicate that share prices are often dominated by whims and fads, by speculators and the so-called Anoise traders.[9]

Several investigators have suggested that the observed increase in the aggregate value of the merging firms is more satisfactorily explained in terms of other theories. Charkham (1989) suggests, for example, that there is at any time a normal share price for a company based on its future prospects, reflecting valuation at the margin. However, when this company is put into 'play', or becomes the subject of an actual or rumoured takeover bid, its price goes up. This does not reflect an increase in the social value of the company's assets, but simply the higher price which has to be paid in order to buy out the intramarginal shareholders for the control of the company. This alternative theory is compatible both with the industrial organisation economists' more or less universal finding, mentioned earlier, of a post-merger decline in profitability and efficiency of merging firms. It is also compatible with another important result in the literature which shows that sometime *after* the merger 'event', the share price of the acquiring company almost always declines.[10]

Takeovers and industrial structure

In assessing the economic effects of takeovers, it is also essential to take into account their impact on the industrial structure. Here the evidence for the advanced countries is ambiguous. In the 1950s and 1960s mergers are generally thought to have contributed to an increase in industrial concentration, both in the US and in the UK. However, in the 1970s and 1980s, despite the big merger wave of the 1980s in both countries, there was little increase in industrial concentration. The reason for this ambiguity is essentially that changes in industrial concentration also depend on a number of other factors (e.g. entry of new firms) which can outweigh the normal concentrating effects of mergers.[11]

Takeovers and short-termism

An important allegation against the takeover mechanism in the USA and the UK is that it encourages short-termist behaviour. At the simplest, the argument is that managers in the Anglo-Saxon firms are obliged to meet the earnings per share target (set by market expectations) every quarter or every half year, depending on the frequency of the stock market's reporting requirements for corporate earnings. If these market expectations of short-term earnings are not satisfied, the firm's share price falls making it vulnerable to takeover. At the same time, on the other side of the market, the investors who are by and large the institutional fund managers are also obliged to have a short-termist outlook. This is because of the highly competitive structure of the fund management industry and the fact that fund managers' own performances are often judged by their principals on the basis of their performances over relatively brief time periods. The net result is a culture dominated by immediate gain and takeover speculation on both sides of the market.[12]

Survey results for the UK indicate that the chief executives of British companies spend an inordinate amount of their time on 'road shows' – making presentations to investors at home and abroad. Similarly, considerable energy is devoted to either avoiding being taken-over themselves, or in planning acquisitions of other companies (Cosh *et al.*, 1990). This distracts from their chief managerial task of creating new products, winning markets and satisfying customers needs in an increasingly competitive global economy. Similarly, there is survey evidence for the USA which indicates high 'hurdle' rates and short pay-off periods for investments by corporations in that country (Porter, 1992).

Experience of Japan and Germany

In examining the merits of the market for corporate control in industrial countries, it is relevant and instructive not only to consider the experiences of the USA and the UK but also to look at those of Japan and Germany. The latter two countries do not have a free market for corporate control in the Anglo-Saxon sense whereby raiders can mount hostile takeover bids against the wishes of the incumbent management. The incidence of hostile takeovers is extremely rare in either country. Odagiri (1994) ascribes the Japanese phenomenon to that country's life time employment system in large corporations. It is also due to the pattern of shareholdings in Japanese companies whereby 75 per cent of a typical corporation's shares are held in 'friendly hands', i.e. the corporation's suppliers, subcontractors and other stakeholders. With only about a quarter of the shares with the general public, it is unlikely that there will be hostile takeover activity. The virtual absence of a market for corporate control in West Germany is attributed by the students of the subject to many factors, including the country's corporate culture,the 1976 co-determination act and employee representation on the corporate supervisory boards, and the concentration of share ownership.

In the context of this chapter a central point is that the lack of a market for corporate control has not in any way held back economic development in these countries. Indeed, the extraordinary post-war success of these economies and their ability to dominate world markets is thought by many to be precisely due to the fact that managers in these countries wee not subject to a constant threat of takeovers. This enabled them to pursue long-term investments, to seek to expand their share of world markets rather than to be concerned with short-term movements in share prices or profits.[13] Particularly important in this respect has been the ability of the corporations in these countries to invest in the training of their work forces. Equally significantly, with a stable corporate environment to which the absence of hostile takeovers make an important contribution, the workers have the necessary incentives to undertake expensive investments in firm-specific human capital, i.e. unlike in the USA and the UK, the Japanese and the German workers could count on their implicit contracts being honoured.

CONCLUSION AND POLICY IMPLICATIONS

The enormous expansion of stock markets in India since 1980 has been a part of a worldwide trend towards deregulation, financial liberalisation and globalisation. The Indian corporate sector has benefited considerably and directly from this evolution which has in a large part been induced by the government's internal and external liberalisation measures. Contrary to *a priori* expectations concerning developing country firms and the capital markets, Indian corporations have been willing and able to raise large sums of money (including more recently foreign exchange) at competitive rates from the stock markets. However, despite this largesse for the corporate economy, it is difficult to detect any gains to the aggregate real economy, at least in the 1980s. During that period there was no rise in the overall savings rate; evidently, all that happened was portfolio substitution by households and institutions from bank deposits to corporate securities. It is also problematic to attribute variations in corporate investments to variations in resources raised from the stock markets, essentially because the latter tended to replace corporations' internal resources, i.e. corporate savings. Nor is there evidence of a more productive use of investment resources. Nevertheless, the government's prudent handling of portfolio capital inflows has ensured that the country did not suffer any serious losses from the surges in such flows which occurred. Thus as far as the progress of the real economy is concerned, despite their extraordinary expansion during the last 15 years, the stock markets so far have been a side-show.

This situation may however change with the market for corporate control, the advent of which would appear to be imminent. As *Business Line* (2 March 1997) reported: 'mergers, takeovers, de-mergers, divestments and de-subsidiarisation have become fairly commonplace on the Indian scene, especially over the last two years'. Left to itself, with the enormous profits to be made on takeovers by merchant banks and other players, there may be sufficient political momentum to enable a fully fledged market for corporate control to emerge within a relatively short time.

The important question is whether the evolution of such a market would be conducive to Indian industrialisation and faster economic growth. The review of the analysis and evidence on the markets for corporate control in the USA and the UK indicate several drawbacks, particularly from the perspective of economic development. First, takeovers greatly intensify the normal stock market pressures towards speculation and short-term returns. Secondly, there is no evidence that the market works in such a way as to always punish the inefficient and unprofitable companies and reward the efficient ones. Empirically, selection in the market for corporate control occurs much more on the dimension of size than that of profitability or the firm's stock market valuation. Thirdly, an active market for corporate control is likely to seriously distort the incentive system facing corporate managers. In Japan and Germany, which do not have markets for corporate control, managers are induced to seek the organic growth of the corporation they work for. In contrast, incentives in the Anglo-Saxon system emphasise financial engineering and growth by merger. Fourthly, in view of the existence of large conglomerate enterprises in India as in many other developing countries, a freely functioning market for corporate control runs serious dangers of increasing concentration of industry as well as stifling the development of small and medium-sized efficient firms. Finally, it is particularly relevant for developing countries to bear in mind the huge transactions costs involved in takeover activity, as well as the very large unfavourable re-distributions of wealth it often leads to (Schleifer and Summers, 1988).

There are serious problems with the present Indian system of corporate governance: conflicts of interest and lack of cohesion among many controlling families, the adverse effects of large interlocking, inter-group investments on small shareholders in the group companies; the total exclusion of ordinary shareholders from decisions with respect to corporate re-structuring, mergers, divestments, etc. It may therefore appear attrative to deal with the whole gamut of such governance problems through the invisible hand of the market – by the institution of the takeover mechanism. However, the evidence surveyed in this chapter from advanced countries suggests that the end result of this whole process may not necessarily be better and could be considerably worse than the current situation. The government should follow the example of Japan, Germany and other countries in Europe and attempt to find other ways of solving these governance problems. A developing country like India simply cannot afford the burden of an extremely expensive, and a hit and miss system of management change which takeovers represent.

The country today stands at an important juncture with respect to questions of corporate governance and of further capital market development. One alternative will be – and unfortunately the one most likely to be followed more by default than by design in the absence of a serious debate – to continue the present drift towards the establishment of the market for corporate control. Another, and the one proposed here, is that the government should take a leaf from the Japanese book and simply not allow such a market to develop.

If the government were to accept the wisdom of the second course, complimentary actions would be required in two important areas. First, the government should take steps to improve the lead bank system which has been in operation in India for the last four decades. This system has not worked as effectively in India as it has in Japan and South Korea. At the theoretical level, there is general recognition of the many advantages of this system relative to a stock market based one. The lead bank system has lower transactions costs and is much better able than the stock market to cope with the problems of asymmetric information and agency costs as well as short-termism. Bhatt (1994a, b) has recently provided an excellent institutional and empirical analysis of the reasons why the lead bank system has been less successful in India than in Korea and Japan. His observations and conclusions would be a useful starting point for a purposive programme for remedying the shortcomings of the system in the Indian context.

The second group of complementary policies in the absence of a market for corporate control would involve stimulating much greater competition in the product markets. In the normal calculus of a capitalist economy, such competition is the main constraint on inefficient managements. In the current Indian context, this would require *inter alia* a fundamental rethinking of the government policies on 'exit'.

In conclusion, this chapter will be a fitting tribute to Dr Manmohan Singh if it leads to a serious discussion on the desirability of the market for corporate control in India: should its evolution be welcomed or, as argued here, should it be regarded as 'a bridge too far' at the present and foreseeable level of development of the Indian economy?

Notes

1. The sources of data presented in this section are Mayya (1993, 1995); IFC (1996); Singh (1997b).
2. Nagaraj (1996) however, suggests that the Indian figures in this paragraph may be somewhat over-stated.
3. These capital account liberalisation measures are subject to restrictions. See further Joshi and Little (1996).
4. The gigantic stock market scam of 1992 focused much public attention on these issues.
5. See, for example, King and Levine (1993).
6. For Brazil see *Acquisitions Monthly* (Nov. 1996); for India see *Business Line* (Mar. 1997).
7. For the UK studies see Meeks (1979); Cosh *et al.* (1980, 1989, 1996); for the US see Schwarz (1982); Mueller (1980); Warshawsky (1987); Ravenscraft and Scherer (1987). For recent review articles see Hughes (1991), Singh (1992, 1993a).
8. See further Singh (1971) and Greer (1986).
9. See further the collection of papers presented in the Symposium on Bubbles, *Journal of Economic Perspectives*, vol. 4, no. 2, Spring 1990.
10. For the US, by as much as 17 per cent two years after the merger. See further Frank *et al.* (1988); Ruback (1988); Hughes (1991).
11. There is a large literature on these issues. It is reviewed in Hughes (1991) and Singh (1992).
12. For a fuller discussion of these issues, see further Singh (1995a). For an opposite perspective, see Marsh (1992).
13. For a fuller discussion of these issues and the survey evidence on managerial objectives in the USA, Germany and Japan see Abegglen and Stalk (1985); Blaine (1993); Kojima (1995) and Singh (1996b).

References

Abegglen, J.C. and G.C. Stalk (1985) *The Japanese Corporation* (New York: Basic Books).

Acquisitions Monthly (November 1966).

Auerbach, (ed.) (1988) *Corporate Takeovers: Causes and Consequences* (National Bureau of Economic Research, University of Chicago Press).

Balasubramanian, N. (1993) *Corporate Financial Policies and Shareholders Returns – The Indian Experience* (Bombay: Himalaya Publishing House).

Bhatt, V.V. (1994a) 'Japan: the main bank system and India: lead bank system', *International Journal of Development Banking*, vol. 12, no. 1, Jan.

Bhatt, V.V. (1994b) 'The lead bank system in India' in M. Aoki and H. Patrick (eds), *The Main Bank System in Japan and Its Relevance for Developing and Transforming Economies* (Oxford).

Blaine, M. (1993) 'Profitability and competitiveness: lessons from Japanese and American firms in the 1980s', *California Management Review*, no. 36, pp. 48–74.

Business line (March 1997).

Charkham, J. (1989) 'Corporate governance and the market for control of companies', *Bank of England Panel Paper*, no. 25, Mar.

Cobham, D. and R. Subramaniam (1995) 'Corporate finance in developing countries: new evidence for india', CRIEFF Discussion Paper Series, n. 9512, University of St Andrews, Scotland.

Corbett, J. and T. Jenkinson (1994) 'The financing of industry, 1970–89: an international comparison', Discussion Paper No. 948 (London: Centre for Economic Policy Research).

Cosh, A.D., A. Hughes and A. Singh (1980) 'The causes and effects of takeovers in the UK: an empirical investigation for the late 1960s at the micro-economic level', in D.C. Mueller (ed.), *The Determination and Effects of Mergers* (Cambridge, Mass., Oelschlager, Gunn and Hain).

Cosh, A.D., A. Hughes and A. Singh (1990) 'Takeover and short-termism: analytical and policy issues in the UK economy', in *Takeovers and Short-Termism in the UK Industrial Policy*, Paper No. 3, Institute for Public Policy Research, London.

Cosh, A.D., A. Hughes, K. Lee and A. Singh (1989) 'Institutional investment, mergers and the market for corporate control', *International Journal of Industrial Organisation*, Mar. pp. 73–100.

Cosh, A.D., A. Hughes, K. Lee and A. Singh (1996) 'Takeovers, institutional investment and the persistence of profits', ESRC Working Papers, n. 30, Mar. University of Cambridge.

El-Erian, M.A. and M.S. Kumar (1995) 'Emerging equity markets in Middle Eastern countries', Paper presented at the World Bank Conference on Stock Markets, Corporate Finance and Economic Growth, Washington, DC, 16/17. Feb.

Franks, J., R.S. Harris and C. Mayer (1988) 'Means of payment in takeover: results for the United Kingdom and the United States', in Auerbach (ed.) (1988) *Corporate Takeovers*: pp. 221–64.

Greer, D.F. (1986) 'Acquiring in order to avoid acquisition', *Antitrust Bulletin*, Spring, pp. 155–85.

Grossman, S.J. and O.D. Hart (1980) 'Takeover bids, the free-rider problem and the theory of the corporation', *Bell Journal of Economics*, vol. 11, pp. 42–64.
Helm, D. (1989) 'Mergers, takeovers and the enforcement of profit maximisation', in Fairburn, J. and J.A. Kay (eds), *Mergers and Merger Policy* (Oxford University Press).
Hughes, A. (1991) 'Mergers and economic performance in the UK: a survey of the empirical evidence 1950–1990', in J. Fairburn and J.A. Kay (eds), *Mergers and Merger Policy*, 2nd edn (Oxford University Press).
IFC (1996) *Emerging Stock Markets Factbook 1996* (Washington, DC: IFC).
Joshi, V. and I.M.D. Little, (1996) *India's Economic Reforms 1991–2001* (Oxford: Clarendon Press).
Journal of Economic Prospectives, vol. 4, no. 2, Spring (1990).
Kojima K. (1995) 'An international perspective on Japanese corporate finance', RIEB Kobe University Discussion Paper No. 45, Mar.
Marsh, P. (1992) 'Short-Termism', in *The New Palgrave Dictionary of Money and Finance* ed. J. Eatwell, M. Milgate and P. Newman (London: Macmillan), pp. 480–6.
Mayer, C.P. (1990) 'Financial systems corporate finance and economic development', R. Glen Hubbard (ed.), *Asymmetric Information, Corporate Finance and Investment* (University of Chicago Press).
Mayya, M.R. (1993) *Indian Stock Markets: Problems, Prospects and Prescriptions* (Bombay Stock Exchange).
Mayya, M.R. (1995) *Reflections on the Changing Scenario of the Indian Stock Markets* (Bombay: The A.D. Shroff Memorial Trust).
Meeks, G. (1979) *Disappointing Marriage: a Study of the Gains from Merger* (Cambridge University Press).
Mueller, D.C. (ed.) (1980) *The Determination and Effects of Mergers* (Cambridge, Mass.: Oelschlager, Gunn and Hain).
Mueller, D.C. (1992) 'The corporation and the economist', *International Journal of Industrial Organization*, vol. 10, June, pp. 700–7.
Mullins, J. (1993) 'Emerging equity markets in the global economy', *FRBNY Quarterly Review*, summer, pp. 54–83.
Myers, S.C. and N.S. Majluf (1984) 'Corporate financing and investment decisions when firms have information that investors do not have', *Journal of Financial Economics*, vol. 13, pp. 187–221.
Nagaraj, R. (1996) 'India's capital market growth: trends, explanations and evidence', mimeo (New Delhi: Indira Gandhi Institute of Development Research).
Odagiri, H. (1994) *Growth Through Competition, Competition Through Growth* (Oxford: Clarendon Press).
Peacock, A. and G. Bannock (1991) *Corporate Takeovers and the Public Interest* (Aberdeen University Press for the David Hume Institute).
Porter, M.E. (1992) 'Capital disadvantage: America's failing capital investment system', *Harvard Business Review*, Sept.–Oct., pp. 65–82.
Prais, S.J. (1976) *The Evolution of Giant Firms in Britain* (Cambridge University Press).
Ravenscraft, D.J. and F.M. Scherer (1987) *Mergers Sell-Offs and Economic Efficiency* (Washington, DC: Brookings Institution).

RBI (Reserve Bank of India) (1995) *Report on Currency and Finance 1994–1995* (Bombay).
Ruback, S.R. (1988) 'Comment' on J.R. Franks, R.S. Harris and C. Mayer, 'Means of payment in takeovers', in Auerbach (ed.) (1988) pp. 137–56.
Schwarz, S. (1982) 'Factors affecting the probability of being acquired: evidence for the United States', *Economic Journal*, vol. 92, June.
Schleifer, A. and L.H. Summers (1988), 'Breach of trust in hostile takeovers', in Auerbach (ed.) (1988), pp. 33–68.
Schleifer, A. and R.W. Vishny (1996) 'A survey of corporate governance', NBER Working Paper Series, n. 5554.
Singh, A. (1971) *Take-overs, Their Relevance to the Stock Market and the Theory of the Firm* (Cambridge University Press).
Singh, A. (1975) 'Take-overs, economic natural selection and the theory of the firm', *Economic Journal*, Sept. vol. 85, no. 339, pp. 497–515.
Singh, A. (1992) 'Corporate takeovers' in J. Eatwell, M. Milgate and P. Newman (eds), *The New Palgrave Dictionary of Money and Finance* (London: Macmillan), pp. 480–6.
Singh, A. (1993a) 'Regulation of mergers: a new agenda', in Roger Sugden (ed.), *Industrial Economic Regulation: a Framework and Exploration* (London: Routledge), pp. 141–58.
Singh, A. (1994) 'How do large corporations in developing countries finance their growth?', in Richard O'Brien (ed.), *The AMEX Bank Prize Essays: Finance and the International Economy, 8* (New York: Oxford University Press), pp. 121–35.
Singh, A. (1995a) 'The Anglo-saxon market for corporate control, the financial system and international competitiveness', University of Cambridge, Department of Applied Economics Working Paper, No. AF16, Mar.
Singh, A. (1995b) *Corporate Financial Patterns in Industrialising Economies: a Comparative International Study*, IFC Technical Paper No. 2 (Washington, DC: The World Bank).
Singh, A. (1996a) 'The stock market, the financing of corporate growth and Indian industrial development', *Journal of International Finance*, 1996, vol. 4, No.2 Fall 1996, pp. 1–17.
Singh, A. (1996b) 'Savings, investment and the corporation in the East Asian Miracle', *UNCTAD Discussion Paper on East Asian Development: Lessons for a New Global Environment*, Study No. 9 (Geneva).
Singh, A. (1997a) 'Liberalisation and globalisation: an unhealthy euphoria', in (eds), Employment and Economic Performance: Jobs, Inflation and Growth (Oxford University Press), pp. 1–35.
Singh, A. (1977b) 'Financial liberalisation, stock markets and economic development', *Economic Journal*, May 1997, pp. 771–82.
Stein, J.C. (1989) 'Efficient stockmarkets, inefficient firms: a model of myopic corporate behaviour', *Quarterly Journal of Economics*, Nov. 1989, vol. 104, pp. 665–70.
Tirole, J. (1991) 'Privatisation in Eastern Europe: incentives and the economics of transition', in O.J. Blanchard and S.S. Fischer (eds), *NBER Macroeconomics Annual 1991* (Cambridge, Mass: MIT Press).
Tobin, J. (1984) 'On the efficiency of the financial system', *Lloyds Annual Bank Review*, July, pp. 1–15.

Warshawsky, M.J. (1987) 'Determinants of corporate merger activity: a Review of the literature', staff study No.152, Board of Governors of the Federal Reserve System, Washington DC, April (1987), summarised in *Federal Reserve Bulletin*, 73(4), April (1987), pp. 270–271.

7 Banks, stockmarkets and financial resources for businesses under the economic reform in developing countries

Jan A. Kregel

The oft-discussed distinction between bank-based and market-based financial systems in providing financial resources for economic development has taken on new importance as the result of the fact that the conditional lending arranged by the IMF for the victims of the Asian financial crisis includes provision which clearly discourage bank-based systems at the expense of increased market discipline. Indeed, many experts consider the primary cause of the crisis to have been the lack of transparency which is thought to be characteristic of bank-based financial systems. However, since most of the difficulties were encountered in the immediate aftermath of rapid financial market liberalisation, the case is perhaps not so clear-cut. Indeed, the problem of the appropriate sequencing of regulations appropriate to a market-based system and the liberalisation of the financial system was first recognised after the crisis in Chile some 25 years ago. The lessons provided by that experience seem not to have been learned, as they have been repeated at increasingly short intervals. But this is true not only of Mexico and Asia but also of the US, Scandinavia and other developed countries. Thus, discussion of economic reforms for the developing countries is perhaps better directed to reform of prudential financial regulation in general, for both developed and developing countries, and for both bank and market-based financial systems.

BANKS VERSUS MARKETS

Indeed, I would argue that the contraposition of banks versus markets as alternative financial frameworks for development represents a false dichotomy that has grown up as the result of a distorted development of financial markets in some European countries after the Second World War. Second, neither banks nor markets are the real source of resources for development. It is now generally recognised that the basic source of finance for business expansion is business savings, that is, retained earnings. Banks provide methods of leveraging these earnings, and stock markets provide owners with the possibility of diversifying the risk associated with holding all their wealth in a single company, but beyond that, there is little to be said for either institution as a source of finance.

Consider two factors. Over the recent past, despite the booms in IPOs as a result of the recent boom, the net contribution of funds raised in the market by industry has been negligible and over some periods negative. Mature firms are buying in their shares, which is a form of returning capital to investors, which is what management is supposed to do if it cannot earn the prevailing risk-adjusted market rate of return (although the justification is usually that the company has the best available rate of return so the management is investing in the company), leaving investors free to invest these funds in the shares of newer companies. But, these newer companies, even if they are brand new, in the sense of having their shares initially offered on the market, must have at least three years of profitable experience behind them, so that they are already in a sense proven companies. Many of them have benefited from 'venture' capital. But, this is also primarily the result of portfolio diversification. Original owners of Microsoft shares are selling their shares and investing the proceeds directly in small companies on the expectation that they might discover the next Microsoft and thus be able to float the company for a large multiple return.

Finally, just as in the early development of the stock market in the US, where the market existed for some 50 years without any appreciable listing for manufacturing companies, but only banks and insurance companies and speculative ventures (I will omit comparison with the London market of the South Sea Bubble), most of the emerging stock markets exhibit the same characteristics. The number of industrial companies quoted is extremely limited, and for the most part the markets are composed of financial companies and property companies. Indeed, this has been one of the explanations for the observed differences between the supposed real rates of return in these countries, and the returns earned in their stock markets which has been decidedly disappointing. None of the high return companies are quoted on the market.

Thus, the stock market remains primarily a liquidity machine, but not an assembler or distributor of real resources. But, banks are also liquidity machines. And the development of stock markets in those countries that are supposed to be representative of 'market-based' systems certainly could not have evolved such systems without the prior development of banks that provide the basic liquidity to the markets. It is a well-documented if little-known historical fact that banks are not created by accumulating real resources that are then channelled to borrowers investing in the highest rate of return projects. Indeed, it is the exception to the rule that bank capital is paid in to create a bank. Usually the promoters obtain a charter for the bank, issue shares to themselves, and then use these shares as collateral for loans that serve to provide the purchase price of the shares. Thus, instead of a bank starting its operations with cash or other real income producing resources on the asset side of its balance sheet to match the liability of equity capital, most banks start out with a portfolio of loans to the bank's owners with bank stock pledged as security. The bank will be capitalised on the basis of the expected future earnings of the bank. But, since these earnings are represented by interest on the loans to shareholders that are at the same time the source of the dividends paid to the shareholders, this is like paying in the bank capital on the instalment plan with future bank earnings. But, banks do not only lend against their own securities, they lend against virtually any and all securities. For example, large US money centre banks have historically been the primary lenders to stock market brokerage firms, and then to broker-dealers acting as specialists. They also lend against fixed income assets. This is still true today, with the government bond repo market representing one of the largest sectors of the US financial market. But, banks have extended this activity to funding the portfolios of large hedge funds as well as stock market specialists and brokerage firms. These market actors could not function, and the equity market could not exist without the support of bank lending.

It is also the case that there has never been a purely 'bank-based' model of development. The industrial development banks that were first instituted in France in the middle of the 19th century, and soon exported to Germany, were shown to be stable only when linked to a viable stock market. This was shown by the experience of Crédit Lyonnais first and then by Banca Commerciale Italiana subsequently. The idea of a successful non-market system in fact comes from the anomalous developments in Germany after the Second World War. But ever here, there has simply been a substitution of the equity market with the fixed income market. The bank bond market now plays a role very similar to that of the equity market prior to the war.

Thus, if a bank creates capital it is by lending capital that it clearly doesn't have and if it lends capital that is has accumulated, it clearly has not provided additional capital. What it creates is liquidity by lending against future business income secured by the current assets of the business. Which is what the stock market also creates by providing markets in which shares can be bought and sold at short notice at prices that do not fluctuate dramatically in normal circumstances. Thus, from the point of view of promoting capital accumulation, neither banks nor markets provide new capital for development. At best, they provide for the circulation of existing capital. It is only to the extent that they provide liquidity that they promote capital development. This leaves the question of whether the provision of liquidity promotes an efficient allocation of resources.

Liquidity and financial market reform

The problem raised by reform is thus not one of the appropriate mix of bank and market – both are required in order to provide liquidity. The question is really one of providing the appropriate reform of the prudential system. In this respect there are two issues. The first is the extent to which allowing unlimited global capital flows is beneficial to the development process and the second is the regulations that should be employed to maximise the benefits.

The history of unlimited capital flows is not a happy one. Indeed, the now abandoned Bretton Woods system was the fruit of the difficulties caused by unlimited capital movements. They were involved in the 1980s Latin American debt crisis, in the 1994 Mexican crisis and in the 1997 Asian crisis. After 1982 debt crisis, much of the blame was placed on commercial banks that had provided the syndicated lending. In order to reduce the reliance on banks in intermediating the flows of funds to developing countries, both market determined portfolio flows and direct investment flows were encouraged.

After the Tequila crisis, the finger of blame was directed to portfolio flows, so that both bank-directed and market-directed flows were suspect. The emphasis was thus placed on direct investment flows, i.e. direct flows within an enterprise or between business enterprises – as Coase has taught us this means bypassing both the market and the bank. The predominance of such investments in Asia was given as example of the stability associated with such flows. Unfortunately, in the aftermath of the Asian crisis, it has come to light that the returns earned on these direct investment flows were unexceptional. In addition short-term commercial bank lending had increased rapidly in Asia from the middle of the decade and the fall off in both was crucial in the propagation of the crisis. The conclusion that must be drawn is that neither banks, nor markets, nor business firms have been especially efficient in allocating capital internationally to its highest risk-adjusted uses.

In all three recent experiences, as already mentioned, much of the blame has been placed on banks. First the developed country banks are faulted for their syndicated lending without adequate risk analysis; banks in the Mexican crisis are faulted for their search for market share rather than return, and finally in the Asian crisis, banks are faulted for their inadequate analysis of risk (although the same criticism should apply to the banks that were lending to them).

It is for this reason that we reach the conclusion that the major problem of the economic reform is the reform of prudential regulation, rather than the form of the financial system. One method of resolving this problem, which has been widely ventilated by representatives of the US government, is to allow free entry to US banks, as well as the right of US banks to take on majority positions in foreign institutions as the result of merger and acquisition. The simple argument is that since the domestic banks need capital, and it cannot be provided domestically, then it must be found abroad. This is the same sort of argument that applied to the privatisation of state property in the former command economies. After the firesale in Central and Eastern Europe there should be another in Asia. Further, since only the banks of the developed countries have the expertise in risk analysis that must be introduced, it would be easier simply to let them apply their systems directly, rather than having locally managed institutions learn how to do it and to train personnel. Of course, the US financial institutions have long been lobbying for free access to developing country domestic markets, first through the Uruguay round, then through the MAI, and most recently by making the IMF responsible for free capital movements. If the case of Mexico is any guide, they need not worry, for the Tequila crisis quickly eliminated any national guarantees contained in the NAFTA treaty.

REFORM AND FINANCIAL MARKET REGULATION

Indeed, the developed countries are currently in the process of revising their approach to financial regulation. In particular, the Basle

Capital Accord is under scrutiny in a number of countries. The basis of the criticisms of the current operation of the Capital Adequacy Requirement is that it refers to 'regulatory' capital, rather than to 'economic' capital. In the words of Alan Greenspan 'the Basle Accord set a minimum capital ratio, not a maximum insolvency probability' (see Greenspan, 1998). Since the formal capital requirements 'do not flow from any particular insolvency probability standard [they] are, for the most part, arbitrary'. The Basle committee has already taken a steps towards self-regulation, allowing banks to use proprietary VAR (value at risk) type models as the basis for calculating the capital requirements to be held against market risks on their 'trading' book (i.e. the assets employed to generate revenue through purchase and sale in the short period) (see BIS, 1997). Studies are also underway to extent this approach to the assessment of credit risks on the 'banking' book (i.e. the assets representing lending at interest).

An alternative, currently under experiment by the Federal Reserve on a sample of large banks, allows them to 'precommit' to an amount of economic capital that their risk management models suggest is adequate. If losses exceed this amount they are subject to sanction by the regulator. The advantage of this approach is that bank supervisors need not be concerned with the particular position of a bank's portfolio, nor with the formal model used to calculate its 'economic' capital. They simply have to monitor the performance of the bank's capital relative to its pre-chosen capital position. If it falls below this figure for a given period, it would suffer a fine and retool its method of calculating its economic capital.

It is perhaps important to recognise that these are the risk assessment systems and prudential regulatory standards that are being proposed for the banks that are to remedy the lax regulatory agencies and bad banking decisions in the countries in financial crisis. It is interesting that a great deal of criticism of the East Asian financial system concerned lack of transparency in financial markets. However, the newest proposals for revision of the Basle requirements leave much of the process to proprietary risk management models that even regulators admit they have difficulty understanding and cannot be considered as transparent to the average bank depositor.

In addition, the fact the banks are increasingly operating their advanced risk management system through what are called leveraged derivative transactions means that there may be even less transparency. Or to put it another way, the kind of transparency that is being called for in Asian banking systems appears to belong to a past age of bank operations. For example, to assess the ability of banks to use and assess common derivative contracts in their risk management strategies, the Bank of England recently completed a survey in which they asked a sample of London banks to price a series of standard derivative packages. It found that (cf. Walwyn and Byres, 1997) the valuations of the derivatives produced standard deviations of as much as 66 per cent of the mean value. For the value of options 'deltas' (that is the change in the price of the option when the price of the asset underlying the derivative changes) that provide the basis for the use of these instruments to hedge risks, the standard deviations reached 20 per cent of the average values for the responding banks.

None of this suggests that the reform of financial systems by allowing the entry of foreign banks will do much to increase transparency, and the ability of banks using these types of risk management systems to prevent financial crisis in the new global financial market based on leveraged derivative transactions remains to be seen. Certainly, the exposure of large financial institutions to merger and acquisition firms, hedge funds and in their own proprietary trading of these instruments does not instill confidence in their ability to bring greater stability and transparency to developing country financial systems.

DERIVATIVES, BANK LIQUIDITY AND REGULATORY REFORM

It has been generally accepted that derivatives played little role in the Asian crisis. However, the quarterly earnings reports of US banks for the last quarter of 1997 suggest a different story, given that nearly all of the losses of the large US money centre banks were reported as related to swaps transactions. Although little is known of the precise nature of these transactions, according to Korean sources, they appear to have been linked to a type of structured credit derivative product first experimented with the Brady Bonds issued to help resolve the Latin American debt crisis.

The basis of a credit swap is for the counter parties to exchange the credit risks associated with an instrument, while retaining the cash flow characteristics. Total return swaps 'enable counter parties to swap the total economic risk attached to a reference asset without actually transferring the asset itself... Under the terms of the swap, Bank B [the beneficial owner of the asset] pays Bank A the cashflows generated by the reference asset, including coupon payments and any appreciations in its capital valued calculated on a periodic mark to market basis. Bank A, in exchange, pays a LIBOR-linked margin plus any depreciations in the capital value of the reference asset' (Ghose, 1997, p. 3). A credit swap or equity swap, eliminates the interest rate risk, but exchanges the credit risk, including the impact of a credit event on the capital value of the asset.

The Brady Bond was the first widely used form that provided the pattern for many of these structured loans to Asian markets. A Brady bond is a structured package in which the developing country (Mexico appears to have been the first) uses its available foreign exchange reserves to create an investment trust vehicle that uses the foreign exchange to purchase long-term, US Treasury, 'zero' coupon bonds. On the basis of these assets, the trust issues its own bonds (which have taken on the name of the former US Secretary of the Treasury who held office at the time) in an amount equal to the maturity value of the Treasury discount bonds. These bonds, which carry the country's sovereign government guarantee, are then swapped for the country's outstanding bank debt, valued at the market discount to face value (it was around 35 per cent in Mexico's case). The principal on the bonds issued by the trust is thus guaranteed by the Treasury bonds and are the holders are thus certain of principal repayment at maturity. The investment trust would also purchase short-term Treasury 'strips' representing only the coupon payments on notes in an amount sufficient to guarantee the first 18 or 24 months of interest payments. From that point on, the interest on the bonds issued by the trust has to be paid from the loans that had been purchased in exchange for the bonds, or from other government sources. The interest on the bonds is thus only partially guaranteed. Banks that exchanged their loans to developing countries in exchange for the bonds could then trade them in the open market, their values determined by changes in the issuing country's sovereign credit rating and in US interest rates which affect the current value of the underlying collateral.

Although the maturities of the Brady bonds were usually 20 or more years maturity, in the case of a bond with a two-year rolling interest guarantee, it was identical to buying a 20-year discount zero coupon bond, a 6-month zero bond, a 12-month zero, an 18-month zero, and a 2-year zero. These streams were default-free, so they could be considered as AAA. It was only the remaining interest payments which carried foreign exchange and sovereign credit risk. According to Watzinger (1997, p. 49):

> An example would be transferring Brady bonds into a trust structure, rearranging the cash flows and swapping them from floating USD into fixed DEM with a bullet repayment. Investors are thus able to achieve a higher yield than a Latin American DEM Eurobond with essentially the same counter party risk. The bank arranging the issue is left with a contingent default risk on the underlying Brady bonds. There can be a loss in the case of a default, as the residual value of the Brady bonds in the trust might not be sufficient to cover the bank's potential loss from unwinding the cross currency swap.

A company set up to buy Brady Bonds could issue 2-year bonds which would be rated AAA since they were backed by US Treasury securities, and another series of bonds with a 20-year guaranteed principal value at maturity and a lower credit rating reflecting the risk on the remaining interest payments. If the rest of the issue could be rated investment grade, the result would have been to transform high risk, impaired, syndicated loans of banks to Latin American governments into low risk investment grade bonds that could be sold to institutional investors, with a profit made from the credit rating differential. This is called credit enhancement, and investment banks quickly extended the Brady principle to other types of developing country debt. Since the first Brady issues were in Mexico (JP Morgan had produced a prototype of the Brady Bond called the Aztec bond in 1988), this extension appears to have also been initiated in Mexico:

> Emerging market borrowers use total return swaps to get access to funding, or reduce the cost of it. The borrower sells assets to a bank and enters into a total return swap. In this swap, he receives the total return on the assets sold and pays Libor plus spread. Consequently, the borrower raises funds while at the same time still being able to benefit from a price appreciation of the asset sold... Investors use total return swaps to get access to their desired emerging market exposure. In a number of countries, severe restrictions in the cash market prevail. For instance, cumbersome settlement procedures, withholding taxes or minimum holding periods. Total return swaps can be an effective means for investors to structure a way around these restrictions.
>
> (Watzinger, 1997, p. 49).

A standard procedure was for an investment bank to create an offshore trust which would buy high interest rate Mexican government issued securities, such as Cetes, which carried an AA credit rating, along with some zero coupon US Treasury bonds. These purchases would be financed through the issue of its own dollar denominated bonds (no longer called Brady's). The bonds could be divided into two classes; one would have its principal collateralised by the Treasury discount bonds in Brady fashion, while the other carried no guarantee. The interest would be paid by the interest generated by the peso asset. For the rating agencies, these were credit enhanced peso bonds, and they were assigned a credit rating equal to the Mexican government rating on its peso issues in the domestic capital market. Since a government security is always the benchmark and thus the domestic risk free rate, it is almost by definition investment grade. The enhanced bonds issued by the trust were thus given an investment grade rating. As dollar bonds paying dollar interest rates they could be sold to US institutional investors. What the investor was in fact buying was a peso denominated Mexican government bond, and the exchange rate risk on the interest payments. But, on their balance sheets these were represented as if they were US investment grade bonds. Again, the result was that US institutional investor funds were being invested in emerging market debt, earning above market interest rates, without their balance sheets necessarily reflecting the actual risk involved. These structures were offered in various combinations, but it still remains true that neither the investor nor the bank intermediary have any direct interest in evaluating either the final use of the funds nor the risk adjusted returns. For the intermediary there was no risk, unless the bank was required to guarantee that it could convert the interest payments into dollars, which only represented a risk if the foreign currency were to become inconvertible (not that it would be devalued, but that it could not be traded at all). This provides one possible explanation of why so much effort was made to prevent Mexico from suspending convertibility in 1994. Structures similar to these were used in Asia (cf. Kregel, 1998) as well as in Latin America. Thus the structured note and the credit enhanced Brady structure provide simple exaples of how funds were moved from developed to developing countries despite the existence of prudential regulatory barriers, and why there was little effort expended in insuring that the funds were moving to the highest risk adjusted return uses. The buyers of the notes were interested in enhancing yield in a low yield environment, while the intermediaries were interested in producing fee and commission income which had no risk and required no Basle Accord capital.

TRANSPARENCY AND STRUCTURED DERIVATIVE CONTRACTS

To see the difficulties that these structures can create for risk management and prudential supervision, consider a variant of the total return swap mentioned above. The emerging market owner of a domestic asset swaps it and its total return (again interest or dividend plus any change in capital value) for a dollar loan equal to the value of the asset and a fixed dollar interest rate. Effectively a US bank is lending dollars against the collateral of an emerging market asset, and the bank is paying the total return on the foreign asset against receipt of a fixed dollar interest payment. Both the bank and the emerging market borrower are facing foreign exchange risk, and the bank is accepting credit risk. For the emerging country borrower the advantage is that the asset remains on the balance sheet and it gains funds at a cost below the domestic market without an entry on the balance sheet and thus no additional capital requirement. It does increase the US bank's balance sheet as it is lending dollar funds. Risk coverage would be arranged by buying the underlying asset, and then financing the purchase through a repo with another bank, thus getting it off its own balance sheet. This hedges the US bank's commitment to pay foreign currency denominated total returns on the asset. This still leaves exchange rate and convertibility exposure on the amount of the loan advanced. This could be hedged by issuing yield enhanced notes for the value of the principal, paying 50 bp over Libor, but which paid interest in foreign currency in the even of a suspension of convertibility (cf the discussion of such structures in Partnoy, 1997).

Since most of these structured products are expressly designed to hide risk exposure by providing credit enhancement, or by being classified off balance sheet, it is not surprising that bank regulators in emerging economies had difficulty in discovering or controlling them. There is no reason why Asian regulators should be more efficient than US regulators who admit to the difficulties. Further, Asian banks were being encouraged, just as US Savings and Loan banks were encouraged in the 1980s, to deregulate, liberalise and to expand their way out of difficulty by investing in higher return market assets. The regulators accepted this argument in the US, it would be difficult to reject it if it were supported by both the government and the multilateral institutions. According to Chew (1997, pp. 54–7), these products 'carried a higher coupon because they contained an embedded short position in ... options. In other words, often when an investor bought a structured note, he simultaneously sold an [exchange]... rate option.... There is no doubt that some less knowledgeable investors did not realize that by buying these securities, they were selling options or engaging in leveraged bets, because some of these features were quite cleverly concealed.... Structured notes are the epitome of how investment technology helped and continues to help money managers circumvent guidelines that were framed to protect the interest of small, unsophisticated investors.

CONCLUSION

Thus, it would appear that much of the liquidity that is currently being supplied to the markets by banks is in the form of structured derivative contracts. Any reform of the domestic financial system will have to take into account the fact that such instruments are commonly used by virtually all banks, and in particular those that are likely to provide the expertise to reform lax banking practices. Their presence and their use of derivative structures will bring radical changes in prudential supervision, and neither their use nor the new methods of supervising them will necessarily increase transparency, nor is it likely to increase stability in either domestic or internal bank flows. Indeed, they appear to eliminate the need for banks to carry risk and thus the necessity to evaluate it appropriately. When fully applied on the international level, this means that if all risk assessment is left to the banks, no one will be evaluating the risk of primary lenders and final borrowers. Prudential regulation may have to extend across borders, or it may have to constrain the cross border flows that are created by such instruments. Currently, most discussion of reform of developing country financial systems rejects either alternative.

References

Bank of England (1997) *The Objectives, Standards and Processes of Banking Supervision*, Feb.

BIS (1997) Basle Committee on Banking Supervision, 'Core Principles for Effective Banking Supervision' (Basle: Bank for International Settlements, Apr.).

Chew, Lillian (1997) *Managing Derivative Risks: the Use and Abuse of Leverage* (New York: John Wiley) pp. 54–7.

G-10 (Group of Ten) (1997) 'Financial stability in emerging market economies', Report of the Working Party on Financial Stability in Emerging Market Economies (Apr.).

G-30 (Group of Thirty) (1997) *Global Institutions, National Supervision and System Risk* (Washington).

Ghose, Ronit (1997) 'What are credit derivatives?', in *Credit Derivatives: Key Issues* (British Bankers' Association).

Greenspan, Alan (1998) Remarks Before the Conference on Capital Regulation in the 21st Century (Federal Reserve Bank of New York, 26 Feb.).

IMF (1998) *Toward a Framework for Monetary Stability* (Washington, DC, Jan.).

Kregel, J.A. (1998) 'Derivatives and global capital flows: applications to Asia', *Cambridge Journal of Economics* (Nov.).

OECD (1991) *Systemic Risks in Securities Markets*, A report by OECD ad hoc group of experts on securities markets (Paris).

Partnoy, Frank (1997) *F.I.A.S.C.O. Blood in the Water on Wall Street* (New York: Norton).

Shapiro, Harvey D. (1997) 'A less dismal science', *Institutional Investor*, Sept. pp. 110–19.

Thieke, S.G. (1997) 'Risk management and the search for increased bank revenue', remarks at the International Monetary Conference, Interlachen, Switzerland, 2 June.

Walwyn, Howard and Wayne Byres (1997) 'The valuation of options', *Bank of England Financial Stability Review*, Autumn.

Watzinger, Hermann, 'Credit derivatives in emerging Markets,' in *Credit Derivatives: Key Issues* (British Bankers' Association).

8 Capital flows and their impact on stability of emerging markets*

Sima Motamen-Samadian and George Croft

In recent years, emerging markets have been subjects of considerable attention. Substantial sums of capital have been flowing in and out of these markets, causing sharp fluctuations in their exchange rate, and upheaval in their economies.

The experience of Mexico and other emerging markets shows that while, initially, the markets appear to be quite stable and attractive to international investors, after a certain stage, they start to exhibit signs of instability and a spiral movement away from the equilibrium. The critical position of the economy becomes evident when both domestic and foreign investors can no longer be convinced of the ability of the market and the government to restore equilibrium. At this stage, to prevent future losses, investors start to move their capital out of the country. The process of capital outflow rapidly gains momentum and accentuates the instability of the foreign exchange market. This would then lead to an acute pressure on the currency to depreciate. In economies where the authorities insist on maintaining a system of fixed or quasi-fixed exchange rate, and try to restore equilibrium by intervention, such pressures lead to rapid depletion of foreign exchange reserves, and eventually force the governments to abandon the existing exchange rate regime.

In all the emerging markets where the above phenomenon was experienced, the flow of short-term capital in the form of portfolio investment have been blamed as one of the main instigators of instability and disturbance. Yet when one considers the behaviour of the well-established markets, one notices that similar large flows of short-term capital do not cause the same upheavals and instabilities in

* This chapter is one of the research outcomes of the Academic Link programme between the University of Westminster in UK and the Universidad Autonoma Metropolitana in Mexico on the project 'NAFTA and structural changes in Mexico'. The programme was supported by the British Council in Mexico.

their economies. One close example of it is the substantial outflow of capital from the European countries to various emerging markets throughout 1996. As pointed out by Scobie (1997), throughout 1996 and 1997, various European banks and financial institutions vigorously engaged in diversifying their portfolios away from the European currencies into the currencies of emerging markets in expectation of the forthcoming EURO, and the possibility of disappearance or a substantial fall in arbitrage opportunities. While it has been argued that the inflow of such large sums of funds into the emerging markets caused overheating in those economies, there were no signs of instability in markets of the countries that exported the capital.

Therefore the question which arises here is what is the main difference between the emerging markets and those of the well-established markets? More precisely, what are the main sources of problem in the emerging markets?:

- Is it the type of the exchange rate regime that is adopted?
- Is it the macroeconomic policies that are implemented?
- Is it the extent of existing outstanding international debt of the emerging markets that makes their economy particularly vulnerable to exchange rate fluctuations?
- Is it the method of disbursement of capital inflows that destabilises the markets?
- Is it the pattern of expenditure and savings behaviour of the private sector that causes the problem?
- Is it the limited capacity of their economy that cannot absorb large inflows of capital and overheats their economies?
- Is it the change in the rate of return of other markets that is the instigator of the crisis?
- Is it the behaviour of the foreign investors who react more violently to the market signals of emerging markets than to those of the well-established markets?
- Is it the behaviour of the speculators who attack the market?
- Is it the fragility of their financial system that cannot cope, with sharp movements of capital in and out of the country?

or

- Is it the mechanism of change in the stability condition of the emerging markets that causes the problems?

No doubt each of the above factors had a role to play in the path to development of crisis in the emerging markets. Indeed, it may be the combination of all of them together which make a market unstable. But in either case, it is important to determine whether these markets are inherently unstable, or there is a mechanism that which changes the nature of stability of the market at some point of time.

If one believes that the markets are inherently unstable, then one should ask why do investors invest in the emerging markets in the first place? Why do they not learn from the past experiences of collapsing emerging markets and keep their funds in a more stable market? Why do they keep coming back to these markets? Are we to conclude that both the international and domestic investors act in a totally irrational manner? Or that they never learn from the past experiences and repeat the same mistakes again and again? Or that they do act rationally, but the rate of return they receive on their investments are high enough to cover the risk premium associated with investment in emerging markets and yet above the return they get from investment in safer markets. But if the latter is true, why is it that the substantial rise in the rate of interest immediately after the crisis does not persuade them to stay in or return to the market that is undergoing a crisis? The reluctance of investors to stay in the same emerging markets immediately after the crisis is a clear indication that the investors are not irrational, and that the rate of return (including the risk premium) is not the only criteria to determine the location of investment. Moreover, the so called tequila effect of the Mexican crisis showed that immediately after the crisis, the international capital remains rather wary of investment in any emerging markets, though after a while they tend to move to some other emerging markets.

Clearly the macroeconomic fundamentals of an economy play a very important role in any decision-making about the location of investment. Indeed acceptable macroeconomic fundamentals of the Asian emerging markets at the time of Mexican crisis in 1994, was one of the reasons which convinced the international investors to move into those markets. But the question, which remains to be answered, is why so soon after the experience of Mexico did investors not hesitate to enter into those markets? After all, Mexican fundamentals also appeared sound when investors first moved into Mexico. This shows that there is also another factor, other than the fundamentals and the rate of return, which plays an important role in deciding where to invest. That is, the perception of the investors as to whether the market exhibits signs of stability or instability. Clearly, if a market exhibits signs of instability then investors would be deterred from entering into that market and if they are already there, they would try to get out of that market. However, if the market shows signs of stability, then even if it were not initially at equilibrium, investors would not be deterred to enter into such a market, as they consider it to be moving towards the equilibrium rather than away from it.

At this stage, one should pause and ask whether emerging markets are always unstable, or they are stable at some stage, but move from one stable condition to another? Recent experiences tend to suggest that there are times during which some of the emerging markets may appear stable but then due to a combination of factors shift from a position of stability to instability. After all the flow of capital into emerging markets indicates that at some stage those markets did show signs of stability and that was why international investors felt confident enough to move into those markets in the first place. Therefore, the question which needs to be addressed is how does a market which appears relatively stable at some point of time, suddenly turns out to be unstable? In other words:

1. What determines the condition of market stability?
2. What is the dynamic of shift from a position of stability to instability?

To answer the above questions, a dynamic model with three asset markets will be introduced to show the conditions of stability of the markets and the factors which may cause a change in the condition of stability.

THE MODEL

The model, which is developed here, is in essence based on the Portfolio Balance model of Allen and Kenen (1980). It includes three asset markets: a money market, a bond market and a foreign exchange market.

It is assumed that the authorities exercise a regime of quasi-fixed exchange rate where there is an upper band on the exchange rate. In other words, there will be no intervention if the exchange rate appreciates below the band, but the authorities intervene should the exchange rate depreciate beyond the upper band. The objective of such an exchange rate regime is to control inflation, which may be caused by depreciation of the currency.

The model is also characterised by a dual economy, where there are two sectors, the traded sector and the non-traded sector. The latter, however, is considered to be a latent sector. Any excess demand for labour in the traded sector can be met by transfer of labour from the non-traded sector to traded sector without any impact on wages. Accordingly, any increase in demand for traded goods and services both domestically and externally can be accommodated without any impact on prices. The combination of the above assumptions allows us to assume prices are fixed. For simplicity domestic prices are assumed to be the numeraire and equal to one. Moreover, the total output is assumed to be fixed though the mix between the non-traded and traded output can change. This implies that while the relative price of non-traded to traded goods may change, the total price index does not change and remains fixed. Now let us consider each market separately.

Money market

Domestic money is assumed to be non-traded, and is only held by domestic residents. In line with Branson and Buiter (1983), and Driskill and McCafferty (1985), stock-flow interaction is introduced through the wealth effects, by making the demand for domestic money and assets dependent upon the level of non-bank private wealth. Private wealth is accumulated and decumulated through the current account surplus and deficits, which in turn affects the exchange rate and the level of private sector wealth. That in turn feeds back into private expenditures and the demand for money.

The model is also based on the assumption that domestic and foreign assets are imperfect substitutes. Hence uncovered interest rate parity condition does not hold. Thus, international investors will hold a diversified portfolio of non-money assets. The proportion of each asset in the portfolio of foreign asset holders depends upon the particular risk-return characteristics of each asset. These particular risk characteristics may include such factors as default risk, exchange rate risk, political risk and differential tax liabilities, all of which serve to drive a wedge between the yields on similar securities.

Having established the above specifications, the supply and demand for money can now be stated as follows:

$$M_t^s = B^a + S_t F^a \tag{1}$$

$$M_t^d = m(r, E\mathring{S}, Y, W_t) \tag{2}$$

or

$$M_t^d = m_r r + m_{\mathring{S}} E\mathring{S} + m_y Y + m_w W_t \tag{3}$$

$$m_r < 0, m_{\mathring{S}} < 0, m_y > 0, m_w > 0$$

where
M_t^s = the stock of money supply at time t;
M_t^d = the demand for money at time t;
B^a = the stock of bonds held by the authority;
F^a = the stock of foreign assets held by the authority;
S_t = the exchange rate at time t measured in terms of domestic currency per unit of foreign currency;
W_t = the private sector's stock of wealth at time t;
Y = the real income;
$E\mathring{S}$ = expectation of future depreciation of currency, where the expectation operator is given by:

$$E\mathring{S} = -\theta(S_t - \bar{S}) \text{ where } 0 < \theta < \infty \tag{4}$$

Also the stock of wealth at time t is represented by:

$$W_t = M_t^s + B_t^p + S_t F_t^p \tag{5}$$

where
B_t^p = The stock of bonds held by the private sector at time t, and;
F_t^p = The stock of foreign assets held by the private sector at time t.

Bond market

In the bond market, the stock of bond supply B is the sum of bonds held by the authorities and private agents at time t and is given by

$$\bar{B}_t = B^a + B_t^p \tag{6}$$

The private sector's demand for bonds is given by:

$$B_t^p = b(r, r^*, E\mathring{S}, \pi, Y, W_t, W^*) \tag{7}$$

or

$$B_t^p = b_r r + b_{r^*} r^* + b_{\mathring{S}} E\mathring{S} + b_\pi \pi + b_y Y + b_w W_t + b_{w^*} W^* \tag{8}$$

$$b_r > 0, b_{r^*} < 0, b_{\mathring{S}} < 0, b_\pi < 0, b_y < 0, b_w > 0, b_{w^*} > 0$$

where
π = the risk premium on private bonds;
r^* = the foreign interest rate, and;
W^* = the foreign wealth.

The total stock of foreign assets at time t is:

$$F_t = F^a + F_t^p \tag{9}$$

Substituting equations (1), (6) and (9) into equation (5), gives the private sector's wealth constraint as follows:

$$W_t = \bar{B} + S_t F_t \tag{10}$$

Substituting for W from equation (10) and for $E\mathring{S}$ from equation (4) into equation (3), gives the equilibrium conditions in the money and bond markets in terms of B^p as follows:

$$B_t^p = S_t[F^a - m_w F_t + \theta m_{\mathring{S}}] - m_r r - m_y Y - m_{\mathring{S}}\theta\bar{S} + \bar{B}(1 - m_w) \tag{11}$$

$$B_t^p = b_r r + b_{r^*} r^* + S_t[-b_{\mathring{S}}\theta + b_w F_t] + b_{\mathring{S}}\theta\bar{S} + b_\pi \pi + b_y Y + b_w \bar{B} + b_{w^*} W^* \tag{12}$$

where equation (11) corresponds to the equilibrium in the money market and equation (12) corresponds to the equilibrium in the bond market.

Foreign exchange market

In this model, it is assumed that decision about the size of imports and exports at period t are made at period $t - 1$ based on the exchange rate at time $t - 1$. Decisions about the capital outflow and inflow, however, are made at time t and are influenced by the expectation of future exchange rate at time t.

In the foreign exchange market, demand for foreign currency comes from demand for imports and capital outflows. Imports in turn are considered to be a positive function of income and a negative function of last period's exchange rate. Capital outflows are negatively related to the domestic interest rate, and positively related to the foreign interest rate, expectation of the future currency depreciation, risk premium on domestic bonds, and domestic wealth. Capital outflows are also considered to be a function of foreign wealth, but it may be either positively or negatively related to foreign wealth depending on the degree of portfolio diversification required and the country risk assessment by the foreigners. In this model, the sign of foreign wealth coefficient though is important in determining the equilibrium level of exchange rate and the foreign assets of the governments does not enter into the condition of stability and hence is not materially important for the analysis of stability. Given the above information, demand for foreign currency may be defined as follows:

$$Q_t^d = g(Y, S_{t-1}, r, r^*, E\mathring{S}, \pi, W_t, W^*) \tag{13}$$

or

$$Q_t^d = g_y Y + g_{S_{t-1}} S_{t-1} + g_r r + g_{r^*} r^* + g_{\mathring{S}} E\mathring{S} + g_\pi \pi + g_w W_t + g_{w^*} W^* \tag{14}$$

$$g_y > 0,\ g_{S_{t-1}} < 0,\ g_r < 0,\ g_{r^*} > 0,\ g_{\mathring{S}} > 0,\ g_\pi > 0,$$
$$g_w > 0,\ g_{w^*} > or < 0$$

where
Q_t^d = demand for foreign currency;
S_{t-1} = last period's exchange rate;
r^* = foreign interest rate.

Note that here it is assumed that foreign prices, the same as domestic prices, are equal to one, i.e. $P^* = 1$.

Substituting for $E\mathring{S}$ from equation (4), and for W_t from equation (10) into equation (14) gives the demand for foreign currency as follows:

$$\begin{aligned} Q_t^d = {} & [g_y Y + g_{S_{t-1}} S_{t-1}] + [g_r r + g_{r^*} r^* + S_t(-g_{\mathring{S}}\theta + g_w F_t) \\ & + g_{\mathring{S}}\theta\bar{S} + g_\pi \pi + g_w \bar{B} + g_{w^*} W^*] \end{aligned} \tag{15}$$

In equation (15) the terms in the first bracket of the right hand side correspond to imports (Z_t), and in the second bracket correspond to capital outflow.

The supply of foreign currency is determined by the demand for exports and capital inflows. Demand for exports is positively related to the last period's exchange rate. Demand for capital inflows is positively related to the domestic interest rate, domestic and foreign wealth, and negatively related to the foreign interest rate, the expectation of future depreciation of the currency and the risk premium on domestic bonds. Here, as mentioned earlier, it is assumed that the exchange rate is quasi-fixed, and the upper band on the exchange rate is given by:

$$S^c = (1+\alpha)\bar{S} \qquad 0 < \alpha < 1$$

where

$S^c =$ the exchange rate ceiling;

$\alpha =$ the percentage by which the exchange rate is allowed to depreciate above the long-run equilibrium exchange rate; and

$\bar{S} =$ the long run equilibrium exchange rate.

It is assumed that as long as the sum of current account CA_t and net capital inflow K_t at the exchange rate S^c is greater than or equal to zero, i.e. $(CA_t + K_t)|s^c \geq 0$, then there will be no pressure on the exchange rate to depreciate beyond S^c, and hence no need for the authorities to intervene in the foreign exchange market. If, however, $(CA_t + K_t)|s^c < 0$, then to prevent depreciation of the exchange rate beyond S^c, the authorities will intervene in the foreign exchange market and sell the foreign currency at the rate of S^c. By doing so, while they run down the foreign exchange reserves dF^a, they keep the balance of payments at equilibrium. Thus the supply of foreign currency is also a function $(CA_t + K_t)|s^c$. Therefore, the supply of foreign currency can be shown as follows:

$$Q_t^s = h[S_{t-1}, r, r^*, E\mathring{S}, \pi, W_t, W^*, (CA_t + K_t)|s^c] \tag{16}$$

or

$$Q_t^s = (h_{S_{t-1}} S_{t-1}) + [h_r r + h_{r^*} r^* + h_{\mathring{S}}(-\theta S_t + \theta\bar{S}) + h_\pi \pi + h_W W_t + h_{W^*} W^*] + h_{F^a}(CA_t + K_t)|s^c \tag{17}$$

$$h_{S_{t-1}} > 0,\ h_r > 0,\ h_{r^*} < 0,\ h_{\mathring{S}} < 0,\ h_\pi < 0,\ h_W > 0,\ h_{W^*} > 0$$

The term in the first bracket of the right hand side corresponds to the exports (X_t), the second term in the square bracket corresponds to capital inflow and the third term corresponds to the change in reserves (dRt), i.e.:

$$h_{F^a}(CA_t + K_t)\,|\,s^c = dR_t$$

and

$$dR_t = -dF_t^a$$

where
dR_t = the way change in reserves appears in the balance of payments;
dF_t^a = actual change in foreign assets of the authorities.

Here it is assumed that h_{F^a} can take two values, (0 and −1) as follows:

If $(CA_t + K_t) \,|\, s^c \geq 0$ or $S_t \leq S^c$ then $h_{F^a} = 0$ and $dR_t = 0, dF_t^a = 0$ i.e. there will be no change in reserves and no change in foreign assets held by the authorities. Therefore, the exchange rate will be determined such that the foreign exchange market clears, and:

$$CA_t = -K_t$$

If, on the other hand, $(CA_t + K_t)| s^c < 0$ or if $S_t > S^c$ then $h_{F^a} = -1$ and $h_{F^a}(CA_t + K_t)| s^c = -(CA_t + K_t)| s^c = dR_t > 0$, where $dR_t > 0$ and $dF_t^a < 0$, i.e. when there is a pressure on the currency to depreciate beyond S^c then the authorities will have to intervene in the foreign exchange market by selling the foreign currency, to keep the exchange rate fixed at S^c. Hence, while dR will be positive to keep the balance of payments accounts at equilibrium, the authorities holding of foreign assets falls.

Note also that:

$$CA_t = X_t - Z_t = h_{s_{t-1}} S_{t-1} - g_y Y - g_{s_{t-1}} S_{t-1} \tag{18}$$

and
Kt = net capital inflow at time t, i.e.

$$K_t = r(h_r - g_r) + r^*(h_{r^*} - g_{r^*}) + S_t[F_t(h_w - g_w) - \theta(h_{\mathring{S}} - g_{\mathring{S}})] \\ + \theta\bar{S}(h_{\mathring{S}} - g_{\mathring{S}}) + \pi(h_\pi - g_\pi) + \bar{B}_t(h_w - g_w) + w^*(h_{w^*} - g_{w^*}) \tag{19}$$

where,
$K_t < 0$ is net capital outflow at time t and
$K_t > 0$ is net capital inflow.

Now substituting for W_t from equation (10) into equation (17) gives the supply of foreign currency as follows:

$$Q_t^s = (h_{s_{t-1}} S_{t-1}) + [h_r r + h_{r^*} r^* + S_t(h_w F_t - \theta h_{\mathring{S}}) + \theta h_{\mathring{S}} \bar{S} + h_\pi \pi \\ + h_w \bar{B}_t + h_{w^*} W^*] + h_{F^a}(CA_t + K_t)) \,|\, s^c \tag{20}$$

In the foreign exchange market, the equilibrium condition is given by equation (21) as follows:

$$
\begin{aligned}
BP = {} & h_{S_{t-1}} S_{t-1} - g_y Y - g_{S_{t-1}} S_{t-1} + r(h_r - g_r) + r^*(h_{r^*} - g_{r^*}) \\
& + S_t[F_t(h_w - g_w) - \theta(h_{\mathring{S}} - g_{\mathring{S}})] + \theta\bar{S}(h_{\mathring{S}} - g_{\mathring{S}}) + \pi(h_\pi - g_\pi) \\
& + \bar{B}_t(h_w - g_w) + W^*(h_{w^*} - g_{w^*}) + h_{F^a}(CA_t + K_t)|\, s^c = 0 \quad (21)
\end{aligned}
$$

Equation (21) gives the equilibrium in the balance of payments. Note that if $(CA_t + K_t))\,|\,s^c \geq 0$ then $h_{F^a} = 0$ and equation (21) will be reduced to:

$$
\begin{aligned}
S_t[F_t(h_w - g_w) - \theta(h_{\mathring{S}} - g_{\mathring{S}})] + S_{t-1}(h_{S_{t-1}} - g_{S_{t-1}}) = {} & g_y Y - r(h_r - g_r) \\
- r^*(h_{r^*} - g_{r^*}) - \theta\bar{S}(h_{\mathring{S}} - g_{\mathring{S}}) - \pi(h_\pi - g_\pi) - \bar{B}_t(h_w - g_w) & \\
- W^*(h_{w^*} - g_{w^*}) & \quad (22)
\end{aligned}
$$

In that case the equilibrium exchange rate will be determined at a level such as $S_t \leq S^c$. If, however, $(CA_t + K_t)|\, s^c < 0$, then $h_{F^a} = -1$, and equation (21) will simply reduce to $S_t = S^c$, and the fall in reserves will be equal to:

$$
dF_t^a = (CA_t + K_t)|\, s^c < 0 \quad (23)
$$

Therefore, the model can be solved for two separate cases. Case I is when there is no pressure on the currency to depreciate beyond the upper band of the exchange rate and hence there is no government intervention. In this case, the stability condition of the model can be determined at a point where all the three markets clear. Case II is when the sum of current and capital accounts at S^c is negative and the government intervenes to prevent the currency to depreciate beyond S^c. In that case, S^c will clear the foreign exchange market, and the stability condition of the model will be determined through the equilibrium condition of the money and bond markets, and the equation which gives the change in reserves. Here we concentrate on the first case.

MODEL SOLUTION

Case I

$$
(CA_t + K_t)|\, s^c \geq 0 \text{ and } h_{F^a} = 0
$$

In this case the model will be solved for a condition when all the three markets are at equilibrium.

From equations (11) and (12) the domestic interest rate r can be derived in terms of the exchange rate, foreign assets held by the authorities and the private sector and other exogenous variables as follows:

$$r = \frac{1}{b_r + m_r}\{S_t[F^a + \theta(m_{\mathring{S}} + b_{\mathring{S}}) - F_t(m_w + b_w)] - Y(m_y + b_y) - \theta\bar{S}(m_{\mathring{S}} + b_{\mathring{S}}) + \bar{B}_t(1 - m_w - b_w) - r^* b_{r^*} - b_\pi \pi - b_{w^*} W^*\} \quad (24)$$

As mentioned earlier, it is assumed that the uncovered interest rate parity condition does not hold due to the presence of the risk premium on domestic bonds. However, it is assumed that the international capital arbitrage ensures that the domestic interest rates will adjust according to the following condition:

$$r = r^* - E\mathring{S} - \pi \quad (25)$$

Substituting for r from equation (25) into equation (24) and substituting for F^a from equation (9) into (24) and rearranging gives the total foreign assets, which correspond to the equilibrium in the money, and bond markets as follows:

$$F_t = \frac{1}{S_t(m_w + b_w - 1)}\{-S_t[F_t^p + \theta(b_r + m_r - m_{\mathring{S}} - b_{\mathring{S}})] - r^*(b_{r^*} + m_r + b_r) + \theta\bar{S}(b_r + m_r - m_{\mathring{S}} - b_{\mathring{S}}) + \pi(b_r + m_r - b_\pi) - Y(m_y + b_y) + \bar{B}_t(1 - m_w - b_w) - b_{w^*} W^*\} \quad (26)$$

Similarly, substituting for r from equation (25) into equation (22) gives the total level of foreign assets, which correspond to the equilibrium in the foreign exchange market as follows:

$$F_t = \frac{1}{S_t(h_w - g_w)}\{S_t[\theta(h_{\mathring{S}} - g_{\mathring{S}} - h_r + g_r)] - S_{t-1}(h_{s_{t-1}} - g_{s_{t-1}}) + g_y Y - r^*(h_r - g_r + h_{r^*} - g_{r^*}) + \theta\bar{S}(h_r - g_r - h_{\mathring{S}} + g_{\mathring{S}}) + \pi(h_r - g_r - h_\pi + g_\pi) - \bar{B}_t(h_w - g_w) - W^*(h_{w^*} - g_{w^*})\} \quad (27)$$

Before proceeding to solve for the equilibrium of all the three markets, let us introduce the wealth constraint and the balance sheet constraints regarding the interest rates and expectations as follows:

$$
\begin{aligned}
&m_r + b_r + g_r - h_r = 0 \\
&m_w + b_w + g_w - h_w = 1 \\
&m_{\overset{\circ}{S}} + b_{\overset{\circ}{S}} + g_{\overset{\circ}{S}} - h_{\overset{\circ}{S}} = 0
\end{aligned} \tag{28}
$$

Substituting for F from equation (27) into equation (26) and incorporating the above constraints gives a first order difference equation in terms of the exchange rate, private holding of foreign assets and exogenous variables as follows:

$$S_t + a_t S_{t-1} = C_t \tag{29}$$

where

$$a_t = \frac{(g_{S_{t-1}} - h_{S_{t-1}})}{F_t^p} \tag{30}$$

and

$$
\begin{aligned}
C_t = \frac{1}{F_t^p}[&r^*(h_{r^*} - g_{r^*} - b_{r^*}) + \pi(h_\pi - g_\pi - b_\pi) - Y(g_y + m_y + b_y) \\
&+ W^*(h_{w^*} - g_{w^*} - b_{w^*})]
\end{aligned} \tag{31}
$$

The solution of the above first order difference equation at time $t = 0$ when $S_t = S(0)$ is given as follows:

$$S_t = \left(\prod_{i=1}^{t} a_i\right)\left[S(0) + \sum_{i=1}^{t} C_i \prod_{j=1}^{i} \frac{1}{a_j}\right] \tag{32}$$

It is difficult to speak of a single equilibrium value (i.e. limit S_t) in this situation as any such point will depend upon all the preceding values of a_i and C_i In other words the equilibrium value, if any, is changing all the time. However, with some simplifying assumptions, it would be possible to state the conditions under which the model becomes stable or unstable. Assuming that the numerator of both of a_i and C_i in equations (30) and (31) are constant, then over time the only variations in a_i and C_i will come from F_t^p in both. In that case, we could write $C_t = Va_t$ where V is a fixed number. Then equation (32) can be written as:

$$S_t = \left(\prod_{i=1}^{t} a_i\right)\left[S(0) + V \sum_{i=1}^{t} \prod_{j=i}^{t} a_j\right] \tag{33}$$

The conditions of stability of the model will then depend crucially upon the value $|a_i|$, i.e. it depends upon whether $|a_i| < 1$, or $|a_i| > 1$. That is because if $|a_i| > 1$, for all sufficiently large i, the term $(\prod_{i=1}^{t} a_i)$ grows without bound, and the value of S_t will tend towards $+\infty$ or $-\infty$. Thus, the market can be considered to be unstable.

If on the other hand $|a_i| < 1$, then for all sufficiently large values of i, as $t \to \infty$, the first term on the right hand side of equation (33), will tend towards zero, i.e. $\prod_{i=1}^{t} a_i \to 0$, while the second term will approach a finite value, which can be viewed as an equilibrium point for the system. Of course, in general, any such value will be influenced by each successive a_i. Hence, the equilibrium point will not be a fixed limit which could be predicted in advance, unless we impose further restrictions on the values the a_i can take. However, since S_t does not show a tendency to diverge to $\pm\infty$, the foreign exchange market can be considered to be stable.

It may also be possible that while initially $|a_i| < 1$, at some point of time, due to change in some exogenous variables it changes to $|a_i| > 1$, in which case the stable model becomes unstable. Similarly, it may be possible for an unstable model to change into a stable model. Let us now consider the conditions of stability.

Stability condition of Case I

As mentioned earlier, the stability of the model requires $|a_i| < 1$. In other words the following condition has to be satisfied;

$$\left| \frac{h_{s_{t-1}} - g_{s_{t-1}}}{F_t^p} \right| < 1 \tag{34}$$

To show the role of capital flows in the stability condition, the numerator of condition (34) has to be rearranged. To do so first note that in the foreign exchange market the imports were represented in the following form:

$$Z_t = g_y Y + g_{s_{t-1}} S_{t-1} \tag{35}$$

Where Z_t represents the imports at time t measured in terms of foreign currency at the rate S_{t-1}. Hence:

$$g_{s_{t-1}} = \frac{Z_t - g_y Y}{S_{t-1}} \tag{36}$$

Similarly the exports X_t measured in terms of foreign currency and at the rate S_{t-1} was shown as

$$X_t = h_{s_{t-1}} S_{t-1} \tag{37}$$

Therefore, $h_{s_{t-1}}$ can be presented as follows:

$$h_{s_{t-1}} = \frac{X_t}{S_{t-1}} \tag{38}$$

Subtracting equation (36) from (38) gives the following:

$$h_{s_{t-1}} - g_{s_{t-1}} = \frac{X_t}{S_{t-1}} - \frac{Z_t - g_y Y}{S_{t-1}} = \frac{X_t - Z_t + g_y Y}{S_{t-1}} \tag{39}$$

Notice that with $X_t - Z_t = CA_t$ and $h_{F^a} = 0$, (as assumed in this case) the exchange rate-while continues to be less than S^c, will change to equate the current account with the capital account, as follows:

$$CA_t = -K_t \quad \text{or} \quad X_t - Z_t = -K_t \tag{40}$$

Now substituting for $X_t - Z_t = -K_t$ from equation (40) into equation (39) and substituting the whole term into the inequality condition (34), gives the stability condition in terms of net capital inflows, domestic income, and private sector's foreign assets as follows:

$$\left| \frac{-K_t + g_y Y}{S_{t-1} F_t^p} \right| < 1$$

or

$$|-K_t + g_y Y| < |S_{t-1} F_t^p| \tag{41}$$

To see more closely when the above condition is satisfied we have to consider three possibilities related to $CA_t = -K_t$.

I.1. $CA_t < 0$ and $K_t > 0$, which implies there is a current account deficit that is matched by net capital inflows.
I.2. $CA_t > 0$ and $K_t < 0$, which implies there is a current accounts surplus that is matched by net capital outflows.
I.3. $CA_t = 0$ and $K_t = 0$, which implies the current account balance is accompanied by zero net capital outflows.

Case I.1

Suppose $CA_t < 0$, and $K_t > 0$, i.e. we have current account deficits matched by net capital inflows. It can be easily shown in this case that $|K_t| < |g_y Y|$.

Now in order for condition (41) to be satisfied, private sector's foreign assets holding measured in terms of last period's exchange rate, has to exceed the sum of net capital inflows and import component of imports.

In other words, when current account deficit is matched by capital inflows, condition (41) is likely to be satisfied so long as private sector's foreign assets is large and exceeds the income component of imports less net capital inflows. If, however, the income component of imports rises rapidly due to some exogenous factor such as a significant rise in income or a rise in marginal propensity to imports out of income, and either net capital inflows cease to rise in line with the above terms, or foreign assets of the private sector starts falling, then the market may become unstable.

This is a condition, that is more likely to occur in economies of emerging markets where the size of private sector's foreign assets may not be very large and sufficient to match the rapid rise in income component of imports. Therefore, to ensure condition (41) is satisfied and market stays stable, capital inflows should keep rising to reduce the size of left-hand side of condition (41). The rise in net capital inflows, however, may lead to some transfer of private sector's foreign assets into the country, and hence reduce the size of private sector's foreign assets, which in turn may change the condition of stability.

It is important to point out that in this model, the change in private sector's foreign assets is not the same as net capital flows, i.e. $K_t \neq dF^p$. That is because capital flows are influenced by both foreign wealth and domestic sector's private wealth. Consequently, a rise in net capital inflows though may be related to some transfer of private sector's foreign assets into the country, and hence indicate some fall in private sector's foreign assets, it may also be due to a rise in foreign wealth without any change in domestic private sector's foreign assets.

Notice also that once the market exhibits signs of instability, capital inflows may fall rapidly and the exchange rate may rapidly hit its ceiling, requiring central bank intervention. That in turn may trigger other exogenous factors which influence capital outflows, and accentuate the instability of the market.

Case I.2

Now suppose $CA_t > 0$ and $K_t < 0$. In other words, net capital outflows are matched by a current account surplus.

In this case condition (41) will be satisfied only if net foreign assets of the private sector exceeds the sum of net capital outflows and income component of imports. If, however, due to some exogenous factors either income component of imports start to rise rapidly or capital outflows rise rapidly and the sum of the two exceed the private sector's foreign asset holding, then the market becomes unstable again.

Here again, a rise in capital outflows though may be associated with some rise in foreign assets of the private sector, the two would not change in the same proportion. Hence a rise in capital outflow, though may lead to a rise in both sides of condition (41), it may not raise the right-hand side as fast as the left-hand side.

Once again the instability condition is more likely to occur in emerging markets where the total foreign assets of the private sector is small and the sudden rise in capital outflows does not lead to an equivalent rise in the domestic private sector's foreign asset holding.

It is also important to note that if the exchange rate starts to depreciate it may continue to do so until it eventually hits the upper band of the exchange rate. That in turn will force the authorities to intervene and prevent further depreciation of the currency. In that case, once again, as before, the stability of the market would have to be determined through the equilibrium condition of the money and bond market.

Case I.3

Finally, suppose $CA_t = 0$ and $K_t = 0$. In that case, the left-hand side of condition (41) will be reduced to the following condition:

$$|g_y Y| < |S_{t-1} F_t^p| \qquad (42)$$

In other words, as long as the income component of imports is less than the private sector's foreign assets measured in last period's exchange rate the market is stable. If, however, condition (42) is violated, due to either an exogenous fall in private sector's foreign assets, or a rise in income, then once again the model may demonstrate signs of instability. This is particularly interesting, because it shows that even when there is no particular concern about current account deficit or surplus, or imbalances in capital flows, in economies where the size of private sector's foreign asset holding is low, the market may turn out to be unstable.

CONCLUSION

The above results, clearly indicate that the economies of emerging markets though may exhibit signs of stability at some point of time, may very well turn out to become unstable as the size of capital outflows increase. Moreover, it was shown that the stability condition of their markets, crucially depend on the relationship between the total level of private sector's foreign assets and the size of net capital flows in and out of the country, which in turn can change various exogenous factors which influences the net capital flows.

References

Allen, P.R. and P.B. Kenen (1980) *Asset Market, Exchange Rates and Economic Integration* (Cambridge University Press).

Branson, W.H. and W. Buiter (1983) 'Monetary and fiscal policy with flexible exchange rates, in J.S. Bhandri and B.H. Putnam (eds) *Economic Interdependence and Flexible Exchange Rates* (Cambridge, Mass: MIT Press), pp. 51 and 85.

Driskill, R.A. and S. McCafferty (1985) 'Exchange rate dynamics with wealth effects, some theoretical ambiguities', *Journal of International Economics*, vol. 19, pp. 329–40.

Scobie, H.M. (1997) 'Implications of EMU for the global emerging markets', *Economic & Financial Review*, vol. 4, no. 3 autumn.